Monbusho Japan.

An Outline History of Japanese Education

Prepared for the Philadelphia International Exhibition, 1876

Monbusho Japan.

An Outline History of Japanese Education
Prepared for the Philadelphia International Exhibition, 1876

ISBN/EAN: 9783337003432

Printed in Europe, USA, Canada, Australia, Japan

Cover: Foto ©Paul-Georg Meister /pixelio.de

More available books at **www.hansebooks.com**

AN

OUTLINE HISTORY

OF

JAPANESE EDUCATION;

PREPARED FOR THE

PHILADELPHIA INTERNATIONAL EXHIBITION,
1876,

BY THE

JAPANESE DEPARTMENT OF EDUCATION.

PREFACE.

The compilation of the following chapters on education in Japan was undertaken as a part of the exhibit of the Japanese Government at the International Exhibition in Philadelphia. They were designed to accompany and in part to explain the collection of articles contributed by the Department of Education. The task of collecting from scattered and obscure sources these records of educational progress, and of selecting from them what might interest the foreign reader, has not been accomplished without some difficulty. The early introduction of letters into a country, the foundation of schools, the encouragement of education by the Government, the growth of literature and a literary class, and, above all, the diffusion of learning among the people, are, to those who desire to understand its civilization, important subjects of inquiry. It is hoped that the account here given in regard to the progress and prevalence of education in Japan may not be without interest, even to those favored Western nations whose science and culture have given them their preëminence.

In the preparation of the following material so many persons have been engaged, that it is difficult to give due credit to all. In addition to those mentioned below, it is proper to acknowledge in this connection the aid of the distinguished Japanese scholar, Rev. G. F. Verbeck, D. D., whose services to education in Japan are well known, who has revised the translations of nearly all the chapters.

The introductory chapter was prepared by David Murray, LL. D., the Foreign Superintendent of Education in Japan, who has also exercised editorial supervision over the publication.

Chapters I. to IV., comprising an account of the introduction and progress of education, were compiled by Otzuki Sinji, with the aid of Naka Michitaka, and translated by Okkotsu Tarotsu.

Chapters V. and VI. were compiled by Sakakibara Yosino, and translated by Suzuki Tada-ichi and Okkotsu Tarotsu.

The Chronicle of Events composing Appendix II. was prepared by Tsumagi Yorinori, secretary to the Minister of Education.

Two explanations are necessary to the reader:

1. In the following pages the Japanese names are printed in the customary Japanese order; that is, the family name stands first, and the individual name, corresponding to the Christian name in English, follows.

2. In translating Japanese words into English, we have followed the system now usually employed by Anglo-Japanese scholars: that is, the consonant-sounds are represented by corresponding English consonants; and the vowel-sounds are represented by the vowels taken with their Italian pronunciation, viz., *a* as in father, *e* like *ey* in they, *i* as in machine, *o* as in note, *u* as in rural. With this key it will not be difficult for the foreigner in most cases to obtain an approximately correct pronunciation.

PHILADELPHIA, *August*, 1876.

CONTENTS.

	PAGE
INTRODUCTORY CHAPTER .	9
Introduction of Learning	10
The Great Schools of Old Japan	11
School-Life in Old Japan	12
Modern Education .	16
Origin of the Department of Education	17
System of Administration .	18
Organization of the Department of Education	18
Elementary Schools	20
Normal Schools	23
Foreign-Language Schools .	26
University of Tokio	29
Professional and Technical Institutions	31
Miscellaneous Educational Agencies .	32
Books and Newspapers	32
Libraries and Museums	34
CHAPTER I.—GENERAL SKETCH .	36
First Establishment of Educational Institutions	38
Foundation of Educational Institutions in Kioto .	41
Works on Law and History .	42
Decline of Learning	44
About the Old Libraries and Schools .	45
Schools of Daimios and Private Schools .	46
Modern School System	47

CONTENTS.

	PAGE
CHAPTER II.—EDUCATION IN THE EARLY AGES	48
Origin of Characters and Books	48
Introduction of Learning, Arts, and Laws	50
Origin and Organization of Institutions for Education, Astronomy, Medicine, etc.	54
Support of Educational Institutions, and Rewards to Professors	61
Regulations of the University	67
Regulations of Provincial Schools	73
Educational Institutions and Libraries at Kioto	78
CHAPTER III.—EDUCATION UNDER THE SHOGUNATE	83
Literary Institutions	84
Rise of the Literary Profession	88
Astronomical Institutions	93
Medical Schools	94
A School of Japanese Language and Literature	95
Early Foreign Scholars	99
Foreign Medical Science	106
Printing under the Shoguns	108
Provincial and Private Schools	109
CHAPTER IV.—EDUCATION SINCE THE REVOLUTION	113
A Year-Period adopted	113
First Educational Measures	114
Reëstablishment of the University at Kioto	115
Publication of Newspapers, etc.	116
Educational Regulations	117
Revision of the Educational System	120
Establishment of a Department of Education	121
An Embassy to Foreign Countries	123
Code of Education	124
Schedules for Elementary and Higher Schools	126
Tokio Public Library	126
Development of the Institutions of Tokio	127
Additional Normal and Foreign-Language Schools	128

	PAGE
Classification of Schools	129
First Report presented to the Emperor	130
Female Normal School	130

CHAPTER V.—JAPANESE LANGUAGE AND LEARNING . . 132

Origin of Japanese Written Characters	132
The Japanese Syllabary	134
Written Characters of the Legendary Age	136
Pure Japanese Characters	137
Composition	139
Metrical Composition	141
Chinese Composition (Kambun)	144
Confucian Learning (Jugaku)	147
Schools	148
Private Schools	149
Examinations and Classification of Honors	150
Penmanship (Shogaku)	152

CHAPTER VI.—JAPANESE ARTS AND SCIENCES . . 154

Drawing and Painting	154
The Medical Art	155
Materia Medica	158
Surgery	159
Doctors of Acupuncture	159
Calendrography	160
Chronometry	161
Kami, or Riyoshi (Japanese Paper)	162
Plants used in the Manufacture of Paper	163
The Manufacture of Paper	168
The Japanese Pencil, or Writing-brush	168
Inkstone	170
Materials for Inkstone	171
Japanese Ink	173
The Engraving of Books	175

APPENDIX.

I. Constitution of the Japanese Department of Education	177
II. Chronicle of Events in the Recent History of the Department of Education	179
III. List of Emperors	187
IV. List of Year-Periods	188
V. Catalogue of the Articles exhibited by the Japanese Department of Education	191

AN OUTLINE HISTORY

OF

EDUCATION IN JAPAN.

INTRODUCTORY CHAPTER.

THE early history of education and literature in Japan, as in all other countries, is obscure and uncertain. In the chapters which follow, an honest and an earnest effort has been made, by competent Japanese scholars, to compile, from all available sources, an outline account of the various steps of progress which have been taken, down to the present time.

To the Japanese student, and to those who are interested in searching into the foundations of Japanese civilization, these annals must present material of the greatest interest and importance.

In the present introductory chapter it is proposed to give a summary statement of the system of education as it existed before the recent revolution, and also of the new system which has been organized and is now in successful operation.

In the theory of the Japanese government, the final and absolute authority is vested in a sovereign ruler called the *Mikado*. An unbroken line of these sovereigns is traced back in Japanese history to about 660 B. C. Penal laws, imperial edicts, and administrative regulations, were all supposed to emanate from the sovereign. From about the twelfth century, however, owing to internal and external commotions, the actual duty of repressing tumults and executing justice upon rebellious subjects was intrusted to a generalissimo of the imperial forces known as the *shogun*.[1] At the beginning of the seventeenth century this office

---

[1] In the early treaties and diplomatic correspondence he is, under a misconception, called *Tycoon*.

fell into the hands of a member of the Tokugawa family, in which it subsequently became hereditary, and so continued down to 1867, when the incumbent resigned the office into the hands of the mikado. During this period of the Tokugawa power, lasting more than two hundred and fifty years, the entire executive authority of the government was exercised by the shogun. He did not, however, assume independent sovereign power, but continued to act nominally as the representative and servant of the mikado.

It was during this period that the feudal system attained its highest development in Japan. The ancient territorial nobles, who were formerly almost independent sovereigns in their territories, were reduced to subjection, and became vassal princes under the shogun. New and conquered provinces were parceled out to the connections of the shogun's family; so that, at the time of the making of the foreign treaties, there were about two hundred of these princes, who, under the name of *daimios*, exercised in their provinces local authority, and yielded to the shogun, as their superior lord, feudal obedience.

Introduction of Learning.—The first steps in education in the empire were taken before the period of the shogunate. China and Corea were in this particular, as in many others, the source from which they derived their first seeds of learning. As early as A. D. 300, there are accounts of Corean and Chinese scholars being brought over to teach a knowledge of the Chinese alphabet and Chinese books to the Japanese imperial court. It is now generally conceded that, previous to the introduction of Chinese, no alphabetical writing existed in Japan. The alphabet of forty-eight characters, known as the Japanese *i-ro-ha*, which is used in the simpler styles of writing, is now considered to have been the modification and simplification of certain familiar Chinese characters. The sounds given to the Chinese characters, when first introduced, were an attempt at an imitation of the original pure sounds as used in the north of China ; but gradually, under the influence of the native speech, they became corrupted and modified, until they could only be understood by sight and not by the ear.

The first teachers employed were brought over from Corea and

China; but subsequently native scholars who had been educated in China were able to take their places, and gradually there grew up in connection with the Imperial Government a system of education which differed widely from its prototype, but was so far fitted to the wants of the Japanese Empire as to secure not only its stability through many centuries, but a high degree of culture and civilization.

The primary object aimed at in the education of this period, which may be termed the "middle ages" of Japan, was not the diffusion of knowledge among all classes of people. This is a conception of recent origin even in Western countries. The object sought was, by means of special training, to prepare men to enter the service of the Government. For this purpose, an institution which we may call a university was established at the capital of the empire. It had branches also in the various principal provinces, which were tributary to the central institution. The subjects of instruction were, in the higher departments, chiefly the Chinese classical writings, which were read and studied by the pupils, and commented upon by learned professors. Special branches of learning which were required in the public service were established as departments of this university. The care of the calendar, and the regulation of the lunar year with its varying months, were confided to a special department, which was responsible for the preparation of the national almanac. Astrology, used for the divination of the future, and medicine, treated in its various branches, in accordance with the Chinese system, were each constituted departments.

This university was supported by the Imperial Government, by means of grants of land, and by assessments upon certain provinces. It passed through many periods of trial and at last perished, but, as the parent institution of the many which sprang up in different parts of the country, it had great influence upon the educational interests of Japan.

The Great Schools of Old Japan.—The founder of the Tokugawa dynasty of shoguns was a liberal patron of learning, and did much to encourage the organization of schools and libraries. He established at his capital, in Yedo, a college which attained great celebrity, and was attended by more than three thousand pupils. It was dedicated to the honor of the Chinese philosopher Confucius. The memorial temple and the statues of Confucius and his disciples are still shown, as objects of interest to those who visit the capital.

Other institutions of a like character were founded by several of the more powerful daimios in their provinces. The Daimios of Mito, Satsuma, Owari, Hizen, Chosiu, Yechizen, and others, vied with each other in maintaining, for the benefit of their subjects, institutions of the highest character. These institutions were, however, designed solely for the use of the "samurai" class, i. e., those who held feudal relations as military retainers to their masters. The children of the common people were not provided for in government schools. The education they received was at private schools, or by private teachers. And it speaks well for the intelligence and love of learning on the part of the merchants, farmers, and artisans, that, even under these unfavorable circumstances, the vast proportion of them could read and write the simpler forms of the language, and could cast up their accounts on the counting-frame. The women also were not educated at the great national schools, but were taught in private schools, or by tutors employed specially for their instruction. The education of females was less extensive and thorough than that designed for boys. They learned to read books in the easier styles, but were not generally taught the Chinese classical authors. They could write and play upon some musical instruments, and were taught female accomplishments in the line of sewing, embroidery, etc. There were, however, some notable exceptions to this limited female education. Female scholars of great celebrity appeared from time to time, and not a few of the most famous names in literature are those of females.

School-Life in Old Japan.—The school-life of the "samurai" boy began when he was about six years of age. His first task was to make after a copy, in weary routine, the Japanese letters. He used at first a brush as large as one's little finger, so that every defect of his execution would be plainly manifest. The master sat by him and directed his movements. Every one of the complicated letters was required to be made with the strokes in the same order, and with the same emphasis. As the cost of paper would be a serious burden, they were required to use the same sheets many times over. The letters of one day were smeared out at its close, and the papers dried in the sun for the next. As you pass along the streets of a Japanese town you may still see the schoolboy's copy-book hung out to dry, and the schoolboy himself you can always detect in his homeward march from school by his smouched fingers and face, which have received more than their share of the writer's ink.

At the lowest estimate a schoolboy was required to learn one thousand different characters. In the Government elementary schools at the present time about three thousand characters are taught. A man laying any claim to scholarship knows eight or ten thousand characters; and those who pass for men of great learning are expected to be acquainted with many tens of thousands.

These characters have each their distinct meaning, so that the learner has not merely to learn the mechanical act of making it, but also its meaning and its proper place and use in a sentence. Many years of the boy's life are mainly spent in this task of learning to write and to use the numerous letters of his alphabet. The earlier reading-books were the simpler Chinese classics, in which the boy was taught the sounds of the characters as well as their meaning. As he advanced, more difficult books were used, and he was exercised, not only in reading the passages, but also in explaining their meaning in the ordinary colloquial style.

Books on manners and etiquette and morals were also used for reading, and were made the text-books for instruction in those branches of education. Up to nine years of age they read without much reference to meaning, and committed to memory some of the standard specimens of poetry. The following were the standard works for early reading:

1. Kokio (The Classic of Filial Piety).
2. Toshishen (Select Poetry of the Tung Dynasty), four vols.
3. Kobun (New Treasures from Old Literature), two vols.

At about nine years of age the boys who were to receive a higher education entered the Chinese Classical Department. In this they were chiefly occupied with the study of the various treatises on Chinese philosophy. The following works, usually taken in about this order, were considered essential; but others were added *ad libitum* for private reading and for special study:

1. Shogaku (Lesser Learning); simple maxims of the sages.
2. Daigaku (Great Learning); a collection of maxims.
3. Rongo (Discourses of Confucius and his Disciples), four vols.
4. Moshi (Discourses of Mencius), four vols.
5. Chiu-yo (The Golden Mean); a treatise on the conduct of human life.
6. Nippon Gaishi (A History of Japan, by Raisanyo).
7. Dai-Nipponshi (A History of Japan prepared under the Daimio of Mito).
8. Shikio (Book of Collected Odes), two vols.
9. Shokio (Record of Classical History), two vols.
10. Shunjiu (Annals of the Shu Dynasty by Confucius), two vols.
11. Reiki (Ritual of the Shu Dynasty), four vols.
12. Yeki (Book of Changes), two vols.
13. Saden (Commentary on the Annals of the Shu Dynasty), fourteen vols.
14. Shiki (Chinese Biographies), twenty-two vols.
15. Zenkanjio (Record of the Kan Dynasty), fifty-one vols.
16. Gokangio (Record of the second Kan Dynasty), fifty vols.
17. Shiji-tokan (Principles of Government), thirty vols.
18. Tokanko-moku (Political History), one hundred vols., etc., etc.

From this formidable list of text-books it is plain that the life of the Japanese college-student was not an easy one. In some schools the course of study was not limited to a definite time, but continued at the pleasure of the scholar. Hence men frequently continued their studies to mature years, like the fellows of an English university. The daily exercises began at about seven or eight o'clock, and continued until about four. There was no vacation except for fifteen days at each of the equinoxes, when the festivals in honor of Confucius were celebrated, and on the prescribed local and national holidays.

The daily routine of a Japanese classical school such as above described would be about as follows: At the opening the students all assembled, say to the number of three or four hundred, in a large assembly-room. Here a professor gave a lecture to the whole body of students on some passage selected from one of the Chinese classics. The lecture consisted of explanations and comments on the selected passages, and of exhortations to the young men to conduct their lives accordingly. Each student was required to have a copy of the book in his hand, and to follow the citations and comments of the professor.

After this general lecture the students retired to separate class-rooms, and there under subordinate teachers read over the works enumerated as text-books. They were required to explain the meaning, and to answer questions to their teacher. On certain days, also, they drew lots to deliver discourses upon some previously-assigned passage. The professors and teachers were held in the greatest reverence, and it was deemed the gravest offense for the scholars to show their impatience or their lack of interest, by yawning, or lounging, or moving their positions. Perhaps to this early severe training, carried on through many generations, are due that wonderful imperturbability of temper and that courtesy of manner which characterize the higher classes of Japan.

Following these exercises were others for teaching them composition, and giving them practice in the art of writing. Official letter-writing was an object of special training, and was carried on through many years. In a country where rank and etiquette, and the proper observance of official forms, were deemed of the last importance, this branch of education was necessarily one not to be neglected. The finer styles of literary composition were matters of ambition with those who desired the highest culture. They were taught to write poetry, not only in the Japanese tongue, but also in pure Chinese. To this day it is a social amusement among their men of culture to turn off impromptu verses, or compose elegant maxims. It is a fair criticism on the system, that time was spent on the comparatively useless accomplishment of versification, which ought to have been employed in increasing their knowledge and in improving their prose composition.

The latter part of the day was spent in physical exercises. As these schools were for the benefit of the military class, the students were trained in martial exercises, such as shooting with the bow and arrow, throwing the lance, running, riding on horseback, and sword-exercise.

Modern Education.—The first seeds of a reformation in the educational system of Japan were sown while the Dutch held the monopoly of trade at Nagasaki. A considerable number of the Japanese learned to speak and to read the Dutch language; and, although the Government discountenanced the introduction of foreign ideas and foreign books, yet both of them slowly percolated into the empire.

The influence of Dutch learning is plainly traceable, especially in the direction of medical science. At the time of the advent of Commodore Perry, in 1853, a very perceptible advance had been made out of the old Chinese medical system into the more rational one of Europe.

But it is only since the country has been open by treaty to foreign trade and foreign intercourse that the influence of Western learning has really begun to affect the national life. The conflicts in which the country was plunged over the question of foreign intercourse led them to investigate for themselves the points in which Western civilization was superior to their own. They could not resist the arguments which were supplied to them in the form of powerful ships with their destructive armaments, the knowledge of military and naval science displayed by the strangers, the many strange and useful articles of manufacture which they brought, and the superior knowledge they displayed in regard to geography, astronomy, navigation, and medicine.

They made early efforts, therefore, to remedy their deficiencies in these particulars. They engaged from France a commission of military officers to instruct them in the modes of warfare in Europe; they purchased vessels, and engaged skilled persons to teach them how to manage them; they bought foreign arms and ammunition for the use of their reorganized troops; they took every opportunity to study the Dutch, English, and French languages, so that they might be able to obtain from foreign books the secrets of that power which they could not fail to acknowledge.

But the most important step was taken when they resolved to send to foreign countries young men to be educated in the sciences and arts of the West. As early as 1861 some of their youth were sent to Holland, and afterward to England and America. Strangely enough, some of the first to be sent out were from provinces whose daimios had been the most bitter opponents to foreign intercourse. They were the first to see that, if they were ever to compete with the power of Western nations, they must be able to turn against them the weapons drawn from their own sciences and arts. The education of Japanese young men in foreign countries, although of so recent a date, has already been productive of the most important results. Many of the most responsible positions in the Government are now filled by the men who received their education and acquired their knowledge of foreign affairs in Europe and America. These men, and others equally enlightened and progressive, saw the necessity of establishing a system of education which should give to their country a knowledge of the languages and sciences of those nations with which in the future they were to be so intimately associated.

Origin of the Department of Education.—Hence, after the revolution in the government by which the shogunate was abolished and the mikado resumed his ancient authority, one of the most important reforms inaugurated was the establishment of a department of public instruction. This took place in 1871, and all matters relating to schools, colleges, libraries, and other educational institutions, were intrusted to this department. The system of education which now prevails, and which is fast providing for the nation a system of universal education, is the work which it has undertaken.

It was not necessary in this work to begin from the foundation. The old system of learning which had prevailed for centuries in Japan, and which had been competent to produce its statesmen and writers and artists, showed, by its results, that it possessed high merit. The traditional fondness and aptitude for scholarship which distinguish the Japanese nation, made it easy to secure the adoption of measures for the advancement of education. Under the stimulus of foreign intercourse, and the strong desire to learn foreign languages, there had already sprung up in various cities schools designed to satisfy this want. As early as 1856 a school for teaching foreign languages was begun in the city of Yedo, under government auspices. Under native and foreign teachers several foreign languages were taught, and the elements of a Western education were supplied. It was out of this nucleus that the present large and flourishing group of institutions for foreign learning in the city of Yedo originated. The newly-organized Department of Education wisely resolved to utilize all such educational material, and has made it the basis for the more systematic and complete set of institutions which it has established.

System of Administration.— In order to understand the system of education devised and established by the department of public instruction, it is necessary to explain something of the mode of administration of the present Government of Japan.

The responsible head of the empire is the mikado, or emperor, in whose name and authority all laws and edicts are issued. The details of administration, however, are intrusted to various departments, each being charged with its appropriate work. These departments are: Foreign Affairs, Home Affairs, Military Affairs, Naval Affairs, Public Works, Education, Finance, Justice, and the Imperial Household. For the purpose of carrying out the details of administration in different localities, the whole country is divided into about sixty kens or *prefectures*, in each of which is organized a local government, the officials of which are appointed by and are responsible to the central Government.

Organization of the Department of Education.—The Department of Education is administered by a minister and other officers. At its organization the head of the department was Oki, a man of great energy and judgment. He was subsequently transferred to the head of the Department of Justice. At the present time the head-officer is Tanaka Fujimaro, the vice-minister. The business is transacted in separate bureaus or boards, each having its appropriate work.

The *Bureau of Superintendence* is charged with the duty of inspecting the schools of the empire, and with the duty of general superintendence. The officers of the bureau are Nomura Sosuke and Hatakeyama Yoshinari, superintendents, together with inspectors and sub-inspectors.

The *Bureau of School Affairs* has charge of the business of the schools with the department, and with the appointment and designation of officers and teachers. The chief officers are Kuki Riuichi and Tsuji Shinji, with whom are associated secretaries and clerks for the transaction of the business.

The *Bureau of Medical Affairs* has charge of the schools of medicine and pharmacy under the department. The health-office was formerly connected with this bureau, but has been recently transferred to the Department of Home Affairs. The chief of this bureau is Nagayo Sensai.

The *Bureau of Reports* collects, arranges, and publishes statistics of education. It gathers information concerning education in foreign countries. It publishes a semi-monthly report containing information for teachers and those interested in education. The compilation and preparation of school-books are in its charge. The chief officers are Nishimura Shigeki and Nakashima Nagamoto.

The *Bureau of Finance* is charged with the care of all financial transactions of the department, with the payment of moneys to the government schools and the distribution of the annual appropriations to the local school bureaus. The head of the bureau is Uchimura Riozo.

The government schools are each managed by a director, who is appointed by the Department of Education, and who is generally one of its officers. The director is responsible for the general conduct of the institution, but in all important matters is required to consult the department.

In each of the local governments there are officers charged with the care of educational affairs, who are required to look after the organization and maintenance of the schools in the different districts. The empire is divided into seven grand school-districts, in each of which it is planned to establish educational institutions for higher instruction. These grand school-districts are subdivided into middle and elementary school-districts. Of the latter there were in 1874 about forty-five thousand. Their boundaries are determined by the natural features of the country, care being taken to construct districts so that the access to the schools may be easy, and also so that the ancient communal associations of the people may be as far as possible respected.

The institutions of learning which have been organized under the department may be classified and described under the following heads:

1. ELEMENTARY SCHOOLS.—The elementary schools are under the immediate charge of the educational officers of the local governments. As fast as the circumstances of the districts would justify they have been established, or where schools already existed they have been reorganized. In this way many private schools have been adopted and have become public schools. A schedule of studies and other regulations for elementary schools was issued by the Department of Education. They are adhered to as far as the condition of the schools and the ability of the teachers will allow. Text-books on the various subjects of learning have been prepared under the direction of the department, and published for the benefit of the schools. Charts for teaching reading, writing, geography, and arithmetic, have been prepared, and instructions for their use have been issued.

The age for admission to the lowest grade is about six years. Males and females are admitted without distinction.

The entire programme of study is designed for eight years, and is divided into two courses—a junior and a senior course, each of four years. Each year is divided into two grades, so that each of the two courses is divided into eight grades, of six months each.

The subjects of study, with the text-books employed, are as follows:

Reading.—Charts of sounds; charts of familiar objects; graded series of readers; lives of western heroes; accounts of official titles and dignitaries, etc.

Writing.—Charts of letters in different styles; copy-books in different styles; official names and titles in Japan, etc.

Arithmetic.—Charts of Japanese and Arabic numerals; addition and multiplication tables; elementary and advanced arithmetic; use of the Japanese counting-frame; elementary principles of algebra; system of Western weights and measures.

Geography.—Maps of Japan; maps of Western countries; elementary and advanced books on geography; books of travels in all countries, etc.

History.—Histories of Japan; history of the treaty-powers; general history.

Morals and Manners.—Doctrines to foster filial obedience; conversations on how to behave; work on virtue, written in pure Japanese; guide to the customs and manners of the world, etc. These subjects are taught orally to the scholars.

Elementary Physics.—First steps in physics; questions and answers in physics for children; physics with illustrations, etc. These subjects are to be taught in part orally.

Physiology.—Elementary physiology and hygiene.

As fast as the wants of the communities require it, secondary schools, graded so as to receive the pupils after they have finished the elementary schools, are to be established. Already in some of the cities this necessity has arisen. The subjects of study are designed to follow those pursued in the elementary schools. They differ from those in corresponding schools in Europe and America in giving more weight to the study of the native language. To read and write this language with correctness and elegance is a much more serious task than in any Western country. Its complicated ideographic alphabet, and its various styles for colloquial, literary, and official uses, render it much more difficult of complete mastery.

The elementary and secondary schools are supported from four different sources: 1. The Department of Education makes an annual grant to all the schools of the empire, in proportion to the school population in each district. The power to make or withhold this grant enables the department to require that the schools shall be conducted in accordance with the regulations prescribed. 2. In most districts the children are charged a small fee, which goes to the support of the schools. 3. A tax is levied in each district, under the supervision of the local school-officers. It varies with the ability of the district, and their willingness to sustain education. 4. Private individuals, especially the former daimios, who still have considerable revenues, and rich merchants, frequently make liberal donations for the support of the schools in their localities.

To show the number and increase of elementary schools the following table is given. The statistics for 1875 are not yet available, but it may safely be stated that the increase has even been greater than that given for 1874. It is estimated that in 1875 the schools numbered at least 30,000, and the pupils 2,000,000.

ELEMENTARY SCHOOLS AND PUPILS.	1874.	Increase for the Year.
Elementary schools, public............................	18,712	10,714
" " private...........................	2,356	
Pupils of elementary schools, male....................	1,303,300	293,684
" " " female....................	421,807	103,471
" " " total.....................	1,725,107	397,155

The following tables give the income from various sources devoted to the support of elementary schools under the direction of the local governments, the expenditures on their account, and the approximate values of their property. The yen is almost identical in value with the gold dollar of the United States.

INCOME OF ELEMENTARY SCHOOLS, 1874.

INCOME FOR 1874.	Yen.	Increase for the Year.
From school-fees.................................	301,603.32	179,650.54
From school-district rates........................	1,458,610.06	620,291.32
From voluntary contributions.....................	1,080,845.46	651,080.78
From government pro-rata appropriations..........	272,330.17	27,804.89
From interest of various funds...................	354,326.50	309,768.76
From miscellaneous sources......................	326,407.50	66,428.40
Total.......................................	3,794,123.01	1,855,024.69

Decrease.

EXPENDITURES OF ELEMENTARY SCHOOLS, 1874.

EXPENDITURES FOR 1874.	Yen.	Increase for the Year.
For teachers' salaries	1,295,686.63	672,540.74
For other salaries	282,527.51	150,516.54
For expenses in inspecting	28,269.64	22,876.38
For building and repairs	643,536.01	351,213.94
For books and apparatus	488,137.25	176,400.45
For fuel and lights	170,832.56	107,657.75
For miscellaneous purposes	286,289.03	138,500.81
Total	3,195,278.63	1,619,706.61

ELEMENTARY SCHOOL PROPERTY, 1874.

APPROXIMATE VALUES, 1874.	Yen.	Increase for the Year.
Value of school-houses	1,038,026.57	505,752.66
Value of school-grounds	124,580.39	74,090.79
Value of school-apparatus	413,595.61	248,346.53
Value of school-books	367,653.63	179,867.85
Amount of school-funds	3,796,392.07	1,936,430.89
Total	5,740,248.27	2,944,488.72

2. NORMAL SCHOOLS.—The chief difficulty, in the introduction of the new methods of instruction and the new subjects of study into the schools, was the want of competent teachers. The old teachers had been accustomed to the old Japanese and Chinese system. Modern arithmetic, the geography and history of foreign countries, and the natural sciences, were comparatively unknown. The first task, therefore, which presented itself to the Department of Education, was the training of teachers for the elementary schools.

In 1872 a normal school was organized in the city of Tokio;[1] it was modeled after similar institutions in foreign countries. An experienced foreigner aided in its organization. It was designed to give the pupils a good education in all the branches to be taught in the elementary schools, and also to give them instruction and training in the proper methods of teaching. This school has now been in operation four

---

[1] At the time of the removal of the imperial capital from Kioto to Yedo, the name of the latter city was changed to Tokio, *i. e.*, "Eastern capital."

years, and has sent out between two and three hundred graduates. It has connected with it a training-school of small children, where the pupils of the normal school are exercised in teaching. It is well supplied with books, apparatus for instruction in physics and chemistry, and with gymnastic appliances. It has a fine building in a beautiful situation, on a portion of the ancient site occupied by the famous College of Confucius.

The course of study extends through two years, and is divided into four grades of six months each. An examination is held at the end of every six months, for promotion into the higher grades.

The subjects of study may be summarized as follows: Japanese and Chinese literature, with practice in writing, reading, and composition; geography, including that of Japan and foreign countries, with exercises in map-drawing and the use of maps and globes; mathematics, including Japanese and foreign arithmetic, geometry, algebra, and trigonometry, with practice in the use of slates and blackboard; the elements of physics and chemistry, illustrated by experiments; physiology, botany, and zoölogy; political economy, ethics, and the principles of government; history, including that of Japan and China, and of the principal Western countries.

The training in methods of instruction begins with the second year. Under a proper instructor they at first observe, and then take part in the teaching of the children in the training-school. They also have a daily conference among themselves and with their teacher, where questions are asked and explanations are given in regard to methods of instruction.

As soon as the success of the Tokio Normal School was assured, it was resolved to establish another in the third grand school-district in the great commercial city of Osaka. It was modeled after the one in Tokio, and its officers and teachers were selected from among those who had been trained in it. One year later the system of male normal schools was made complete by establishing five others, thus giving one to each grand-school district.

Female education had never received that attention in the old system of education that its importance deserved. The wise and progressive statesmen of the present era saw the necessity of giving to female education a great and a decided impulse. This purpose was secured by the enlightened generosity of the empress, who resolved to do something to promote the education of her own sex. She gave from her own private purse the money necessary to erect a building for a Female Normal School, and directed the Department of Education to see her wishes carried out. An excellent building was thereupon erected on a beautiful and commanding site, and in October, 1875, it was dedicated in the presence of her Imperial Majesty, with simple but impressive ceremonies. It was immediately opened for the instruction of female teachers, and is now in successful operation.

The graduates of the normal schools were, as rapidly as they could be turned out, sent into the various kens to assist in reorganizing the elementary schools in accordance with the new regulations. Under the direction of the local school-officers, they have in a variety of ways aided in spreading a knowledge of the new system among the old teachers. Sometimes they have done this by going round from school to school, explaining and illustrating the methods of teaching and showing the use of blackboards and charts and books. Sometimes they have established at some central point a model school, where all the improved appliances are put into use, and where the old teachers come and observe, and receive explanations from the normal graduates. And finally they have in many kens been employed to organize a kind of local training-school, where the teachers of the ken are gathered together, and not only receive instruction in the methods of teaching with the improved appliances, but also are taught the simpler elements of the subjects which are to be introduced into their schools. At the present time there are not less than fifty of these local training-schools in the different parts of the empire.

Of course, it is well understood that these improvised teachers are very imperfectly fitted for their work, and only serve a temporary purpose. Yet the plan has been successful in establishing schools on a more extensive scale than could have been possible in any other way.

Although the instruction must for a long time to come be imperfect, yet the progress has been both substantial and rapid beyond all expectation.

The following table gives a summary of the government and local normal schools as they stood in 1874. Since that time great progress has been made. Additional local normal schools have been established, and the Female Normal School, with one hundred and fifty students, has been opened.

A TABLE SHOWING THE SCHOOLS FOR TRAINING TEACHERS.

NORMAL SCHOOLS IN 1874.	NUMBER.		Number of Teachers.	Number of Students.
	Governmental.	Local.		
First grand-school district...................	1	17	95	1,477
Second grand-school district..................	1	6	58	1,079
Third grand-school district...................	1	4	33	547
Fourth grand-school district..................	1	6	36	529
Fifth grand-school district...................	1	4	16	233
Sixth grand-school district...................	1	6	22	773
Seventh grand-school district.................	1	2	25	384
Total.......................		52	285	5,022

3. FOREIGN-LANGUAGE SCHOOLS.—For the present, and possibly for a long time to come, the higher education of the Japanese must come to them through a foreign tongue. Their own language is too deficient in the literature of foreign science, and even in well-understood terms for the expression of the ideas of foreign learning and philosophy, to make it a fit medium for their communication. Just as, in the middle ages of Europe, the Latin was employed as the learned language, so for the present, at least, the Japanese must employ the English as the language in which they must study science and philosophy. At a later period, when a set of men have been trained in all the learning of the West, and are capable of drawing continued inspiration from foreign books, they will in turn interpret these ideas to their countrymen. They will coin the new words, write the new books, teach the new sciences, which shall put Japan and Japanese literature on a level with the civilization of Western nations.

To effect these results, the Department of Education has established at important centres schools for foreign learning. In each of the seven grand-school districts a school of this character is established, to be conducted in the English language. In addition to this there is in Tokio a school in which are taught German, French, Russian, and Chinese. An English school for girls has also been in operation for several years in Tokio.

The programme of studies in these language-schools extends through six years, and is divided into a junior and senior course, each of three years. The students are admitted to these schools after they have finished the junior course of the elementary schools, and in addition have acquired such a knowledge of the foreign language that they can read and speak easy sentences.

The studies of the junior course include the following subjects:

JUNIOR COURSE.

Japanese Language: Daily training in reading, writing, and composing.

English Language: Daily drill in the pronunciation, spelling, reading, and conversation, followed by grammar and the art of composition.

Writing and Drawing.

Geography: Native and foreign; map-drawing; use of maps, globes, etc.

Mathematics: Arithmetic; practice in mental computation; elements of algebra.

History: Japanese and Chinese history, and an outline history of Western countries.

Morals and Manners: Oral instruction.

SENIOR COURSE.

In addition to the above subjects the following are studied:

Mathematics: Geometry, algebra, and trigonometry.

History: The history of the several countries with which Japan is connected by treaty.

Physics: The elements of general physics and chemistry.

Natural History: Including botany, zoölogy, and physiology.

Philosophy: Including the elementary principles of ethics and metaphysics.

Political Science: Including discussion of the different forms of government, the principles of political economy, and of international law.

Besides the government foreign-language schools, there are a large number of private schools, taught in a great part by native teachers, in which, however, sometimes foreign teachers are employed. For the year 1874 eighty-two such schools are reported as in operation.

In connection with schools of foreign languages it is proper to mention the important influence upon education produced by the schools, established in connection with the various foreign religious missions in Japan. Before the establishment of the present government schools, they were almost the only means by which a knowledge of foreign languages could be obtained, and many of the best foreign scholars received their first instruction in the schools of missionaries. At the present time there are many schools of this kind both for males and females. A careful estimate made for me a year ago gives the number of scholars under the instruction of the Protestant missionaries as not less than seven hundred. Those under the missions of the Greek and Roman Churches must be a still greater number.

FOREIGN-LANGUAGE SCHOOLS.

FOREIGN-LANGUAGE SCHOOLS IN 1874.	NUMBER.		Number of Teachers.	Number of Students.
	Governmental.	Local.		
First grand-school district	2	56	147	3,631
Second grand-school district	1	8	29	348
Third grand-school district	1	11	23	655
Fourth grand-school district	1	..	5	55
Fifth grand-school district	1	1	6	68
Sixth grand-school district	1	2	32	304
Seventh grand-school district	3	4	5	258
Total	10	82	247	5,319

4. UNIVERSITY OF TOKIO.—To provide for the higher education in this national system, the Department of Education has begun by establishing in the capital an institution of a high grade. It grew out of the old foreign-language school which was founded in 1856, and which has been developed step by step as the wants of the country demanded. It is designed as the receptacle for those students of the various foreign-language schools who desire to obtain a professional or a technical education. Its present university organization was effected in 1873.

The requirements for admission are a proficiency in the studies of the junior course in a foreign-language school. That is, the applicant must possess a thorough knowledge of the English language, both as to writing and speaking. He must be a good elementary Japanese and Chinese scholar. He must have mastered arithmetic, descriptive geography, and the history of Japan, as well as an outline history of Western nations.

The programme of studies extends through six years, three of which are devoted to a general course of study in fundamental subjects, designed to give general culture as well as a preparation for the separate special courses which are to follow. During the last three years the students enter upon professional or technical subjects, being divided into separate departments or colleges for that purpose.

The general course includes the following subjects:

Language: Grammar; rhetoric; English literature; logic; with practice in English composition.

Mathematics: Algebra; geometry; trigonometry and its applications.

History: General history; history of England and her colonies; of the United States; France and Germany; history of civilization.

Physics: Elements of physics, with experimental illustrations; general inorganic chemistry, with practical illustrations; descriptive and physical astronomy.

Natural History: Human and comparative anatomy and physiology; botany; botanical physiology; zoölogy; mineralogy; geology.

Political Economy: History and principles of political ethics.

Latin: Grammar, and exercises in translation into English.

The special courses are pursued in distinct colleges, in which the students, besides continuing certain general studies in science and philosophy, are chiefly occupied with special and professional branches. It is a part of the plan of this university to increase the number of special departments as the circumstances may demand. At present the following schools are organized and in operation :

1. *College of Law,* in which the pupils study the Latin and French languages ; the philosophy of mind and morals ; the history and science of politics ; international law ; English law ; Roman law ; French law ; comparative jurisprudence, especially as applied to the penal and civil laws of Japan.

2. *College of Chemical Technology,* in which the pupils study the French language ; the philosophy of mind and morals ; mineralogy, geology, and mining ; physics, with laboratory practice ; general chemistry ; analytical chemistry ; chemical technology ; and metallurgy.

3. *College of Engineering,* in which the studies are the French language ; the philosophy of mind and morals ; physics, with laboratory practice ; mineralogy, geology, and mining ; higher mathematics ; land and railway surveying ; hydraulic engineering ; theoretical and applied mechanics ; thermo-dynamics ; machines ; designs for engines and engineering works ; drawing, and graphical calculation.

4. In addition to the foregoing departments of study, there is a *School of Arts and Manufactures* conducted in the Japanese language. The studies are divided into two courses, viz., a course in chemical arts and a course in mechanical arts. Each course extends through three years, of which one year and a half is employed in preparatory studies, and the remaining one year and a half in special studies and technical work. The studies include the following :

Chemical Arts: Arithmetic ; algebra ; physics ; chemistry ; laboratory practice, and practical training in the manufacture of chemical products.

Mechanical Arts: Arithmetic ; algebra ; geometry ; drawing ; physics; chemistry; mechanics; experiments with machines, and practical training in the manufacture of mechanical products.

It may be mentioned that the greater part of the philosophical apparatus in the educational part of the Japanese exhibit was manufactured at the School of Arts and Manufactures.

The chief director of the university is Hatakeyama Yoshinari.✗ The instructors are in part foreigners and in part Japanese. The following statistics will exhibit the present condition of the institution:

Directors	2
Other officers	11
Foreign professors	20
Japanese professors and instructors	14
Students in School of Law	17
Students in School of Chemistry	24
Students in general course	131
Other students	156
Total students	349

The university has a library of books, chiefly text-books and books of reference, for the use of professors and students. The collections of apparatus in physics, chemistry, and engineering, are extensive and practically serviceable. It has also a good working collection of minerals, and geological and other specimens.

5. PROFESSIONAL AND TECHNICAL INSTITUTIONS.—The want of trained public servants led the Government, at an early period of its foreign intercourse, to establish institutions to provide men educated and trained in the special arts of the West. It was under the pressure of this necessity that the following institutions have been organized and put in operation:

1. *Military College.*—This was established first in 1867, under the care of a French military commission, detailed for this purpose from the French army. It is doubtless due to this commission, and to the instruction given in the military college, that the Japanese army has attained its present high degree of discipline and efficiency.

2. *Naval College.*—The success of the army school led to a subsequent organization of a similar kind for the navy. The instruction is in

✗ Died, Oct. 20/76.

the English language, and is given by a commission of officers detailed from the English navy.

3. *Engineering College.*—To supply competent engineers for its operations, the Department of Public Works has established a college. The students are taught the English language, and receive a thorough course of instruction in theoretical and practical engineering. The graduates from this college are appointed to positions in the various divisions of work conducted by the department.

4. *Medical College.*—Medical education was always a subject of care on the part of the Government, and, when the impulse toward foreign education began to be felt, medicine was one of the favorite new sciences. The result òf the efforts toward medical education was the establishment of a medical college of a high character. It is conducted in the German language. Already its influence is felt in 'the progress and improvement of medical practice in the country. Instead of the old empiric Chinese system, there is a strong tendency to adopt the more scientific methods of Western practice.

In estimating the progress that has been made in medical education, we must not omit the organization of hospitals in the empire. Of these there are now a large number located principally in the great cities. In most of them one or more foreign physicians are employed, and in all such cases a class of medical students is connected with the hospital, who receive systematic instruction as well as daily practice among the patients of the hospital.

6. Miscellaneous Educational Agencies.—Schools and colleges are by no means the only agencies by which the education of a nation is advanced. The circulation of books and newspapers, and the establishment of libraries and museums, are now everywhere recognized as exerting an important influence upon the progress of human knowledge. Of these influences it is important to give some account in any statement of the agencies which are now promoting education in Japan :

1. *Books and Newspapers.*—From an early period a class of literary men existed in Japan. They were held in high esteem, and usually were the pensioners of the General Government or of some one of the

territorial nobles. The ancient literature of Japan consisted mainly of works on history and philosophy, together with poetry, and works of fiction. The introduction of the art of printing with blocks enabled printers to multiply books at a moderate cost. Works of fiction were extensively read by all classes, especially by females. Under the impulse created by the opening of the country to foreigners, a strong desire sprang up to obtain a knowledge of foreign countries and foreign laws and customs. It may be safely asserted that the new literature in Japan is now chiefly directed to the supply of this want. Thousands of books have been written and published in reference to foreign countries. Many important works have been translated, both for the supply of the popular demand and for the information of the officers of the Government. Educational books have been extensively compiled or translated from foreign sources, covering most of the subjects of elementary instruction in the schools. Dictionaries and other books facilitating the acquisition of foreign languages have been prepared.

The newspaper, in the present sense, is a new institution in Japan, dating back only about nine years. The design in its first establishment was, to provide a means of explaining and defending the progressive measures which the Government had adopted. Since that time newspapers have multiplied rapidly, so that now there are more than one hundred in different parts of the country. In the capital alone there are at least a dozen, many of which have a large circulation, two at least reaching ten thousand daily. The best literary talent of the day is employed upon these newspapers, and subjects of public and international interest are discussed with a force and intelligence which will bear comparison with the best journalism of the times. There is a bureau for the regulation of the press, and occasionally unpleasant collisions have occurred, but in the main a large degree of liberty is allowed by the Government, and a hearty support is tendered by the press.

The necessity of making the newspaper intelligible to the various classes of readers has produced a marked modification in the style of writing. The stiff, learned Chinese style, affected by the old admirers of the classics, has given way to a more near approach to the language of the people. It is believed that this modification will become a permanent improvement to the language, and will render the diffusion of knowledge more rapid and easy.

2. *Libraries and Museums.*—From the time of the recent transformation of the Government, the collection of books has become necessary for the use of the departments and the institutions of learning. The first public library, however, under the new *régime*, has been opened in the capital by the Department of Education. It was first organized in 1872 and then contained only Japanese and Chinese books. In 1875 it was reorganized on a larger basis and now contains a valuable collection of foreign as well as native literature. The leading periodicals, both in Japanese and foreign languages, are kept on file. It is free to the public, and is designed as a general library, to be annually increased by the expenditure of a stated sum.

In 1873 a museum was organized, intended to exhibit the following classes of collections: Industrial specimens; specimens of art, and art applied to industry; specimens of scientific and educational apparatus; specimens in natural history, agriculture, and ethnology. This museum grew out of the collection of articles made for the Vienna Exposition, and has gradually increased, until it is now a collection of rare value and interest.

Another museum has been more recently organized by the Department of Education, for the benefit chiefly of the educational institutions located in Tokio. It is, however, also intended to be opened for the public benefit. It is less a general museum than a special series of collections in the various subjects important in an educational course.

The two tables which follow, and which close this chapter, will furnish some statistics in reference to the attendance at the various grades of schools and the number of teachers employed. The population as given in the table does not include that of the northern island, Yezo, nor the Liu Kiu Islands. These dependencies are not included in the seven grand-school districts, and the administration of their educational affairs is not intrusted to the Department of Education:

TABLE SHOWING THE POPULATION AND NUMBER OF PUPILS IN 1874.

Population of seven grand-school districts	33,579,909
Whole number of pupils	1,739,422
Percentage of pupils to population	5.18
Pupils in elementary schools	1,725,107
" " " males	1,303,300
" " " females	421,807
Pupils in government and local normal schools	5,022
Pupils in foreign-language schools	5,319
Pupils in government colleges	3,927

TABLE SHOWING THE NUMBER OF TEACHERS IN 1874.

Whole number of teachers	38,365
Whole number of male teachers	37,731
Whole number of female teachers	634
Teachers in elementary schools	37,611
Teachers in normal schools	285
Teachers in foreign-language schools	247
Teachers in government colleges	245
Foreign teachers	212

CHAPTER I.

GENERAL SKETCH.

IN the earliest times the use of alphabetical characters was unknown in our country, and was introduced when intercourse with foreign countries was first opened. Characters are said to have been first introduced by natives of Mimana, a part of the present Corea, who visited our country during the successive reigns of the Emperors Kaika and Suijin (157 B. C., 30 B. C.).

Books were first introduced into this country by the Empress Jingo (200 A. D.), who brought them from Corea, which country she invaded with naval forces in the reign of the Emperor Chuai (192 A. D., 200 A. D.).

The first use of writing for public affairs seems to have been in the reign of the Emperor Richu (400 A. D., 404 A. D.), when officers of the finance department were appointed to keep accounts of receipts and expenditures, and officers were also appointed in each province to record and report all the affairs of the local governments.

The son of the Emperor Ojin (270 A. D.) was taught to read the Chinese classics and histories, under the instruction of a professor called Wani, who was sent from Corea to the imperial court, in the sixteenth year of the reign of the emperor.

This was the commencement of the study of literature in this country.

Although the art of weaving is said to have been originated by

Tensho-daijin, the commencement of its general practice dates from the reign of the Emperor Ojin (270 A. D.), who called weavers and needle-workers from China, by sending messengers thither for the purpose. The Emperor Yuriyaku (457 A. D.) again called such artisans from abroad and distributed them to all the provinces.

After this period these arts began to be extensively practised.

As to the medical art, it owes its origin to Oanamuchi-no-Mikoto, and Sukuna Hikona-no-Mikoto.

Subsequently, the Emperor Jukio (412 A. D.) sent for physicians to Shirako, one of the states of Corea.

The Emperor Ninken (488 A. D.) sent for carpenters to Koma, also one of the states of Corea.

The Emperor Keitai (507 A. D.) invited professors to teach the Chinese classics from Corea, and the Emperor Kinmei (540 A. D.) sent for professors of medicine, almanac-making, and divination. At this time Buddhism was also introduced. In the reign of the Empress Suiko (593 A. D.) a priest of Corea, named Kanroku, came and presented to the empress books on almanac-making, astronomy, and geography. In the twelfth year of her reign almanacs were first used. At this period an embassador was first sent to the court of the Zui dynasty of China, and the ceremony of opening intercourse with that court was performed. After the Zui dynasty was superseded by that of To, the practice of sending embassadors to that court was still kept up.

A student named Takamuku Kuromasa, and a priest called Bin, returned hither after having been educated in China. In the first year of the reign of the Emperor Kotoku (645 A. D.) these two persons were appointed professors, and were directed to assist in the administration of government.

This is the first instance of political honor being bestowed upon scholars.

During the reign of the Empress Suiko (593 A. D.), the Prince Shotoku administered the government, and, while he was thus acting as regent, he established seventeen regulations as the fundamental laws of the country. These are, however, scarcely anything more than mere instructive maxims.

The prince being a most devoted believer in Buddhism, exerted himself to promote its doctrines; so that from this period it became predominant in the country.

The Emperor Kotoku, who was fond of learning, effected a change in the system of government. He enforced a just and equal administration in all the provinces, and remedied the abuses of the local officers by appointing new governors of provinces in the place of the old ones, who had virtually held the lands and their inhabitants as their own property and subjects.

In the second year of his reign, the emperor established new laws, the rules of administration in the provinces and counties, the enumeration of the population, the rate of taxes, and the measurement of lands. He also encouraged good government by rewarding merits and punishing crimes, and promoting extension of education.

At this period Prince Tenji, who afterward became emperor, acted as regent, as the Prince Shotoku had formerly done under the Empress Suiko.

First Establishment of Educational Institutions.—The first educational institution was founded in the second year of the Emperor Tenji (668 A. D.), who established at the seat of government a national university, with its professors and students. In the fourth year of the reign of the Emperor Tenmu (672 A. D.) an observatory was erected for the observation of the position and movement of the heavenly bodies. In the first year of Taiho (702 A. D.) the emperor effected a great change in the educational system, by reorganizing the university in the capital and establishing provincial schools in each province, and a superior school in Dazai, the principal seat of government in the island of Kiusiu. Departments of medicine and astrology were also established in the government, to superintend all matters concerning these sciences in all the provinces.

In the university, professors of the sounds of the Chinese characters, of penmanship, of medicine, of the treatment of diseases of women, of almanac-making, and of astronomy, were appointed, and students were chosen to be educated in each of these sciences. A musical department was also established, with teachers of music to instruct pupils both in the old national music and in foreign music.

When the penal laws and the imperial edicts were first codified in the first year of Taiho (702 A. D.), rules of education were also established, defining the duties of professors and the studies of students. By these rules, the full term of study for students was fixed at nine years, and the books to be used in instruction were arranged in three grades, viz., senior, middle, and junior. The ages of students to be admitted were limited from thirteen to sixteen in all branches of education. But the educational system in those days was not designed to diffuse knowledge among the people at large, but merely to provide from among the students persons to be employed in public offices. Particular rules of examination, therefore, were adopted, according to which students who obtained the first or second degree in the examination were regarded as having successfully passed the examination. They were again subdivided into six classes, according to the grade attained in the examination.

In the first year of Keiun (704 A. D.) a certain allowance was made for educational purposes out of the public fund reserved to meet general exigencies.

In the first year of Tenpeihoji (757 A. D.), and again in the thirteenth year, public land was appropriated for the encouragement of education. Besides these grants, there was another appropriation made in each province. This was rice collected as interest on loans made to farmers, and was appropriated to pay for provisions and other miscellaneous expenses of students.

Expenses for study were first allowed to Sugawara Kiyogimi by the Emperor Kanmu (782 A. D.). This was called "the monthly allowance;" and since that time this has always been allowed to the children of the Sugawara and Oye families, when applied for.

The Empress Jito (690 A. D.) rewarded professors by giving them a revenue from the produce of land, from silver, or from landed property.

Subsequently this practice of rewarding men of learning was constantly kept up through successive reigns. In the first year of Tenpeihoji (757 A. D.) the students, who were appointed professors or physicians in the provinces, were ordered to present their first year's salary to their former teachers.

In the fifth year of Showa (838 A. D.) this proportion was altered ; and in the eleventh year of Jokan (859 A. D.) the rate to be thus surrendered was fixed at one-tenth of one year's salary annually, and this was made the permanent rule.

The subjects of instruction were divided into four courses, as follows : The course in which history was taught, together with the art of composition ; the course in which the six Chinese classics were studied ; the course in which the penal laws and the imperial edicts issued as rules of action were taught ; and the course in arithmetic and mathematics. Besides these, there was a course in the sounds of the Chinese characters ; and one in penmanship.

In the medical department there were four separate courses, viz. : in the treatment of internal diseases ; the treatment of incised wounds and of skin-diseases ; the treatment of diseases of infants ; and the treatment of diseases of the ear, eye, mouth, and teeth.

Besides these, the arts of shampooing, of acupuncture, and of applying moxa, were taught, each as a separate branch of study.

In the astronomical department the movements of the sun, moon, and stars, were observed. Astrological divination was taught and practised, and the annual number of days, etc., was computed for the almanacs.

As to the method of choosing students, those of the university were to be selected from among the children of families which were entitled to adopt the term Shi (literature) for their family name, and only from those above the eighth rank. Students of the medical department were chosen from among the children of families entitled to adopt the term Yaku (medicine) for their family name, and from among those of the families hereditarily professing medicine. Students of astrology were chosen from among the children of the families adopting the term Boku (divination) for their family name, and from among those of families hereditarily professing that calling.

In the fifth year of Jinki (728 A. D.) the professorships of law and composition were established in the university, and students were admitted to be educated in these branches of study. Those students who made distinguished progress in the study of the arts or sciences were chosen to form a distinct class, called Tokugiosei (fellows). A rule was established in the eighth year of Yenriyaku (789 A. D.) by which students of the university below thirty years of age were excluded from public employment; but this rule was abolished in the first year of Tencho (824 A. D.), and students of all ages were admitted into the public service, according to their talents and knowledge.

Foundation of Educational Institutions in Kioto.—In the thirteenth year of Yenriyaku (794 A. D.) the Emperor Kanmu founded the castle called Heianjo at Kioto in Yamashiro, and established near it an imperial university. Subsequently the Sugawara and Oye families founded schools, within the grounds of the university, consisting of two buildings, called the eastern and western halls.

Fujiwara Fuyutsugu, a minister of state, established a school on the southern side of the university for the education of the children of the Fujiwara family.

The consort of the emperor, Saga, also founded a school for the education of children of her family, namely, that of Tachibana.

The Prince Tsunesada converted a building used as a pleasure-house of the emperor into a school for the education of the children of the O family. Ariwara Yukihira also founded a school for the O family.

These five schools were originally private institutions, but afterward were incorporated as branches of the university.

With regard to the libraries, during the period Hoki (770 A. D., 780 A. D.), a person called Isonokami Iyetsugu collected books for the use of the public.

During the period Yenriyaku (782 A. D., 805 A. D.), Wage Hiroyo founded a library, in which he kept several thousand books.

Sugawara Michizane also collected a library.

A large number of books were accumulated by the Oye family, and, as they had been preserved through many successive generations without being destroyed by fire, Oye Masafusa once remarked that the literary calling descending by inheritance in his family shared the same fate as the imperial court. This remark proved to be true, for, when the library of the Oye family was subsequently destroyed by fire, the imperial court also declined.

Fujiwara Yorinaga, a minister of state, who was very fond of literary pursuits, purchased a great number of books, which he arranged in the four classes of Chinese classics, histories, miscellaneous, and Japanese books, and placed them on shelves, distinguished from one another. The greater part of the books were of his own copying.

Works on Law and History.—The laws and regulations of Japan were formerly divided into the following classes, viz.: The penal laws; the imperial edicts, issued as rules of action; incidental regulations adopted from time to time to meet the exigencies of the moment; and official instructions prescribed for the government of officers in conducting their affairs. Although these were all originally copied from the laws adopted by the To dynasty in China, it was by the Emperor Tenji (668 A. D.) that they were first established in this country. These were again arranged by the Emperor Tenmu (672 A. D.) and were afterward revised by the Emperor Monmu (697 A. D.), during the periods of Taiho, under the name of Taihorio. The Empress Gensho (715 A. D.) again revised this work during the period Yoro. This was called Yororio, and consisted of twenty-seven volumes, two of which are now lost. The penal laws consisted of twelve volumes, of which only four are now extant.

The incidental regulations were completed during the three successive periods, Konin (810 A. D., 823 A. D.), Jokan (859 A. D., 876 A. D.), and Yengi (901 A. D., 922 A. D.). This work consisted of thirty-two volumes, of which nine are preserved. The official instructions established in the period Yengi, consisting of fifty volumes, are entirely preserved. The two codes of rules established in the period Konin and Jokan are embodied in Yengishiko.

The commencement of the compilation of histories dates from the twenty-eighth year of the reign of the Empress Suiko (620 A. D.), when Prince Shotoku, with the assistance of Soga Umako, compiled the history of the emperors, and a history of the country.

They were left unfinished, and, being kept in the house of Umako, when his son, Yemiji, having suffered punishment for his crimes, set his house on fire and destroyed himself, the history of the emperors, together with other works, was reduced to ashes.

A person called Funeno Eshiaka saved the history of the country from destruction by the same fire, and presented it to Prince Nakano Oye.

The Emperor Tenmu having formed the intention of compiling a history, ordered in the tenth year of his reign the Princes Kawashima and Oshikabe to prepare a history of the imperial reigns, with other events of former times. The two princes died before the work was completed. The Empress Genmiyo ordered the Prince Toneri to superintend the work, which was finished in the fourth year of Yoro (720 A. D.), and is entitled "Nihonshoki" ("A History of Japan"). This is the first history of this country, and was soon followed by others, such as "Zokunihonki," "Nihonkoki," "Zokunihonkoki," "Buntoku-jitsuroku," "Sandaijitsuroku," "Honcho-seiki," etc. All these are authentic histories of this country.

For more than seven hundred years after these works were written, no important historical writings appeared. Works of an historical nature were published, but they were far from being correct and complete. Mitsukuni, the Prince of Mito, having in his youth cherished the design of completing a history of Japan, wrote a work commencing from the reign of the Emperor Jinmu down to the time when the two imperial courts became united into one. His son Tsunayeda (1702 A. D.) prosecuted the intention of his father and completed the history after the lapse of one hundred years from the death of Mitsukuni.

This history is called "Dainihonshi" (or, "History of Great Japan"), and consists of two hundred and forty-two volumes, including the chronological record of events and biographies of particular persons. Though it is to be regretted that notes and chronological tables have not been added to this history, still it is considered to be the most complete ever written in this country.

Decline of Learning.—From the period of Yenriyaku (782 A. D., 805 A. D.) perfect tranquillity prevailed in the country during one hundred years. Literature was much cultivated through the successive reigns, and many talented and learned men flourished. At this period literary culture reached a standard never before attained. But, as prolonged peace is apt to produce effeminacy in life and indolence in literary pursuits, the result was that at last educational institutions also began to be less successfully managed than before.

Miyoshi Kiyotsura (914 A. D.), who possessed practical ability and political knowledge, presented to the emperor, in the fourteenth year of Yengi, a memorial containing twelve articles, in which, among other things, he stated his opinion on the subject of education in the following words : " The successful government of a country depends upon wisdom, and wisdom depends upon education.

" Now, educational institutions have been allowed to become places of hunger and cold, in consequence of the insufficient maintenance received from the land-tax and from the income of the farmers' rice-loans which, in the course of a long period, have come to be not so well-managed as formerly. It is humbly requested that the educational land-tax be restored to its former condition, and that the income from rice-loans be applied to the support of students ; and it is further requested that strict orders be given to professors to recommend students to the imperial service in the most impartial way."

It is seen, from what is mentioned in the code of rules established in the period Yengi, that his request was complied with.

A work containing a code of regulations, and consisting of fifty volumes, was completed and presented to the emperor in the fifth year of Tencho (927 A. D.). It is seen from this work that the literary and political institutions at this time were in a very satisfactory condition. There is one volume called " The Rules of the University," which describes the ceremonies to be observed at the festival given in honor of Confucius, and the rules in regard to the lectures given by professors, and also the rules for examining the students, as well as the regulations for the allowance to be made for their support.

The decaying condition of the university is referred to in the statement of Fujiwara Atsumitsu, who presented his memorial on seven subjects to the emperor in the first year of Hoyen (1135 A. D.).

When Yorinaga, councilor of state, superintended the examination of students in the third year of Ninpei, he examined them in his private residence.

In the first year of Jisho (1177 A. D.), the ceremony of the festival given in honor of Confucius was performed in the office of the Imperial Government, the university having been destroyed by fire. From these facts it will be seen that the university was then in a decaying state.

About the Old Libraries and Schools.—A library was founded by Hojo Akitoki (1240 A. D.), and is located in the village of Kanazawa, in the province of Musashi. The institution was used as a school during the nine generations of the Hojo family, and a number of books, both Chinese and Japanese, were kept in it. Some of the books are to this day found scattered among the people. A school was established in the village of Ashikaga, in the province of Shimotsuke. It was a provincial school in the middle ages of Japan, and when it decayed it was turned into a school for priests of the Zenshu sect of Buddhists. During the period Onin (1370 A. D.), Uyesugi Norizane rebuilt the school-house, stored books in it, and endowed it with lands. As literature was entirely neglected, and became almost extinct at this period, owing to the general disturbances and agitations, this was the only school existing in the whole country, and is said to have been resorted to even by students from the western and northern parts of the country.

Tokugawa Iyeyasu (1603 A. D.) instructed Hayashi Doshiun to establish a school, but owing to some cause the work was not accomplished. In the seventh year of Kanyei (1630 A. D.) a school was first established under the government of Tokugawa on the Uyeno hill. In the period Genroku, Nobuatsu, the grandson of Doshiun, removed the institution to the site of the Temple of Confucius, when it was called the Shohei School. Doshiun, the grandfather of Nobuatsu and Shiunsai, his father, both kept their heads shaven, and were classed among the Buddhist priesthood. Nobuatsu, however, abandoned the priesthood, and allowed his hair to grow, and received the title of Chancellor of the University.

By the time that Hayashi Ko Dainaiki represented the family three generations after Nobuatsu, literature became extensively cultivated.

Tokugawa Iyeyasu (1603 A. D) regretting the destruction of books which had taken place during the long wars and disorders, took measures to encourage the printing of books. For this purpose he instructed Hayashi Doshiun to purchase useful works. He employed every means to obtain them, and had them printed as he found them.

In the thirteenth year of Keicho (1608 A. D.), he used types in printing, and in the nineteenth year he is said to have used copper types. Printing was first used as early as in the reign of the Empress Koken (749 A. D.), when "Mukuseijokio," a sacred book of the Buddhists, was printed; but since that time no mention is made of printing books for the space of nearly four hundred years, till the third year of Shoan (1301 A. D.), when "Gokenho" was printed. This is the commencement of printing in the middle ages of Japan.

"Hanniyakio," a sacred book of the Buddhists, was printed in the first year of Genriyaku (1184 A. D.). "Sentakushu" was printed in the second year of Kenriyaku, and "Shiorioshiu" was printed in the second year of Shoka (1258 A. D.). Since this period the art of printing has been extensively practised, so that a second edition of "Rongo," the Confucian Analects, was printed in the period Shohei (1347 A. D.). The art of printing with types was early practised, but the precise date is not known.

Schools of Daimios and Private Schools.—After the period of Genna (1615 A. D., 1623 A. D.), when general peace and order were established under the Tokugawa family, each Daimio became possessed of his own land, and provided for the education of his vassals, and the people living in his dominion. The first school ever built by a Daimio is the one founded by Kobayokawa Takakage (1580 A. D.), but the oldest school among those which have remained until recent times is the one established by Uyesugi Kagekatsu (1596 A. D.). Next to those persons comes Mayeda, the Prince of Kaga, who did much for the spread of literary learning, and erected a large school called Meirindo. Besides these schools, there were many similar establishments in Owari, in Higo, in Aidzu, etc. Ikeda, the Prince of Bizen, built a school at Shibutani, to educate his vassals in literature as well as military science. Among all others, the two schools of Mito are most conspicuous.

A school founded by Ito Jinsai (1680 A. D.) is the first school ever founded by a private individual. Since then nearly all who professed classical or literary learning have had their private schools. In the period Bunka (1801 A. D., 1817 A. D.), Nakai Sekijen established a school at Osaka. This was the largest private school in recent times.

Modern School System.—At the restoration of the imperial government (1867 A. D.), the management of educational matters was again resumed by the Imperial Government, and many changes were introduced. In the fifth year of Meiji (1872 A. D.), the Educational Department was established. The country was then divided into seven grand school-districts for educational purposes. These districts were again subdivided into districts for higher schools, and into districts for common schools. Educational regulations were established, and courses of study laid out, and required to be taught in the schools of the country. A normal school and a school of the English language were also established in the principal seat of each of the large educational districts. A medical school and hospital were founded at Tokio. At the University of Tokio various sciences and arts are taught in the English language. Schools for the instruction in foreign languages, and those for the education of females, have been established, together with normal schools for the education of female teachers.

Technical schools for military and naval science, for engineering, for medicine and law, have been organized and opened. So that at least the most pressing educational wants of the country have been provided for.

CHAPTER II.

EDUCATION IN THE EARLY AGES.

Origin of Characters and Books.—The education of the people being the foundation of good government, it has never been neglected by those who have aimed at promoting the prosperity of a country, and the happiness of its people.

To furnish, therefore, the means of education to every youth in the country, by providing schools and teachers of various branches of knowledge, forms one of the most important and necessary measures to be adopted by the state.

In the earliest times the use of characters was not known in our country, and tradition was the only means by which the deeds or words of the ancients were preserved and transmitted. Nor did the use of characters become known till intercourse with foreign countries was opened. The use of this important medium of knowledge is said to have been introduced by a native of a country called Okara (one of the ancient provinces of Corea), who visited this country during the reign of the Emperor Kaika (157 B. C.).

Subsequently, in the reign of the Emperor Shuijin (97 B. C.), another person of the same country came to live in Japan who is believed to have aided in the introduction of a written language.

In the reign of the same emperor, an envoy was sent to the imperial court by the King of Okara to pay tribute; and again, in the sixty-eighth year of the same reign, the royal prince of the same country came to pay his personal respects to the imperial court, and entered the service of the Emperor Shuijin (97 B. C.), who thereupon gave the name of Mimana to the prince's native land. From this time foreigners began to pay visits to this country, and it is believed that the art of writing dates from this period, although the national histories furnish no clear evidence on this point.

There existed at a later period a book consisting of five volumes, under the title of "Hijinsho." This book was written by Hijin, who, although it is not clearly proved, is said by some to be a native of Koma, in Corea; but the work is now lost, and but a few of the characters used in it are extant.

The Emperor Chuai (A. D. 192) died while on an expedition against Kumaso, who had been instigated to revolt against the imperial authority through secret communications made by the people of Sankan (the present Corea), a country consisting of the three states, Shiraki, Koma, and Kudara, situated in the neighborhood of Mimana.

An envoy from Mimana to Japan, sent to pay tribute, was also robbed by the people of Corea.

These acts of the people of Corea led the Empress Jingo (A. D. 200) to undertake in person a naval expedition against that country. After having conquered the country, she seized the magazines within the capital, and returned with all the writings and books found in them. She then established a branch of the government of Japan in Mimana, to preserve order and peace in Corea. Since these periods our country began to be constantly visited by foreign embassadors, who came to pay tribute, and thus characters and writing came into general use.

The Emperors Ojin (A. D. 270) and Nintoku (A. D. 313) were both fond of literary pursuits, and greatly patronized them. The Emperor Richu (A. D. 400) caused the accounts of receipts and expenditures in the department which had charge of the precious metals, jewels, and other valuable things of the emperor, to be kept in writing, and appointed Wani and Achino-omi, natives of Kudara, for this purpose. The emperor, in the fourth year of his reign, appointed recording officers in each province to record all the proceedings of the local government, that the wishes of the people of all quarters might be known to the imperial court. This is the origin of the appointment of recording officers in the provinces as well as in the court. Thus the utility of writing and of books began to be manifest.

Introduction of Learning, Arts, and Laws.—In A. D. 270, the youngest son of the Emperor Ojin, when a mere boy, being very fond of reading, endeared himself to his father, and was by him nominated his heir.

In the fifteenth year of his reign, a son of the King of Kudara, in Corea, named Ajiki, came to this country, and, being a great scholar in the Chinese classics, was made tutor to the prince.

Once, being asked by the emperor if he knew any professor superior to himself in learning in his country, Ajiki nominated Wani, saying that he was the most learned man in the whole country. Upon this the emperor immediately sent for Wani, who came the year following and presented to the emperor the book of "Confucian Analects," and also the "Thousand-Character Classic."

The prince read many books and made great progress in his studies under the instruction of Wani, so that upon one occasion, when a letter was sent to the emperor by the King of Koma, his knowledge enabled him to detect uncivil terms in the letter, which he tore up, severely reproving the envoy who had presented it. Wani passed his life in this country in the service of the imperial court.

From Wani descended two families with whom literature became an hereditary profession. The posterity of these two families increased in number, and lived respectively in Yamato and Kawachi. They were called eastern and western families, Yamato being situated in an eastern and Kawachi in a western direction.

In the seventh year of the reign of the Emperor Ketai (A. D. 514) a professor of the five classical books was invited from Kudara, in Corea, by the order of the emperor. A professor was accordingly sent from Kudara, and in the tenth year of the same reign another came to succeed him in his office.

This is the commencement of the practice of calling professors from foreign countries to educate students in literature.

In the twenty-fourth year of the same reign, the emperor issued a decree ordering that the selection of men for the public service be made to depend upon their integrity and learning, so as to encourage the cause of morality and education.

This is the origin of the custom of appointing students to the imperial service from the university and from the provincial schools, and for a long time this was the fundamental principle of the educational system in Japan.

After a time, Kotoku-Bateian, professor of the five classical books, came from Kudara to succeed Koanmo in his office, and in the fifteenth year of the reign of the Emperor Kinmei (A. D. 540) another professor named Oriuki again came and succeeded them in the office.

Oshinji, the descendant, in the fifth generation, from Wani, pursued his hereditary profession, and was employed by the Emperor Bitatsu on account of his literary talents.

Once he displayed his ability in reading a letter presented to the emperor from Koma, which none among the literary families was able to make out. Upon this the emperor much praised his talent, and requested him to attend always near him, while he reproached the others for their imperfect learning. About this period Buddhism found its way into this country, and gained many converts among all classes of people. The study of literature from this time fell largely into the hands of the priests, and the practice of calling scholars from Corea to fill the office of professors of literature was no longer kept up.

In the reign of the Empress Suiko (A. D. 593), the Prince Shotoku assisted her as regent in the administration of the government.

This prince had a strong memory, and acquired an extensive knowledge, but, being a most devoted believer in Buddhism, considered the promotion of the religious cause the most important affair of the government of the country. He did not, however, entirely neglect the encouragement of education, and therefore, in the thirteenth year of the same reign, sent an envoy to the court of the Zui dynasty in China, together with two students, named Takamuku and Minamibushi, and the priest Bin, to be educated there. These students remained there for ten years, until the Zui dynasty was superseded by that of To.

Takamuku remained more than twenty years longer, but the priest and Minamibushi returned sooner. The latter gave instruction to the Prince Nakano Oye (afterward the Emperor Tenji) and to Nakatomino

Kamako (better known as Fujiwara Kamatari), who afterward aided in destroying the rebellious Soga Emiji and his son.

The Emperor Kotoku, on his accession to the throne (A. D. 645), made the Prince Oye heir-apparent, and promoted Kamako to the rank of chief privy councilor.

The emperor was a great patron of literature, showing favor to all men of letters without distinction of position.

He appointed Takamuku and Bin to the professorships of the provincial schools, giving them a share in the administration of the Government. This is the first instance of natives being appointed to professorships, which had hitherto been occupied exclusively by scholars from Corea.

The arts of weaving and sewing were introduced into Japan by Achino Omi. He was the descendant of a king of the Kan dynasty, in China, who fled to the northeastern frontier of the country on the fall of the dynasty. He lived in a region adjoining Corea. On this account he became acquainted with this country, and in the twentieth year of the reign of the Emperor Ojin came hither to settle, accompanied by inhabitants of all the seventeen provinces.

All the people whom he brought with him, both men and women, were intelligent and well-practised in the arts of weaving and sewing. In the thirty-seventh year of the same reign Achigimi was sent to China to procure more weavers and sewers. After the lapse of five years he returned with four female weavers, whom he presented to the Emperor Nintoku, the last emperor having died in his absence.

This is believed to have been the first introduction of these arts into Japan.

The cultivation of mulberry-trees, however, was not carried on at these periods. Their introduction dated from the reign of the Emperor Yuriyaku (A. D. 457), who, being attentive to the interests of the people, was anxious to introduce the culture of silkworms. To attain this end he induced the empress to engage in this occupation, in order thus to lead the people.

In the fourteenth year of the same reign the emperor again sent for weavers and sewing-women from China by dispatching a special messenger for that purpose; and on their arrival distributed them to the several provinces. Mulberry-trees were planted in all places whose soil was suitable to their cultivation. From this period the arts of weaving and sewing began to be extensively practised.

The medical art was introduced in the second year of the reign of the Emperor Iukio (A. D. 412), who sent for a physician from Corea to cure his sickness. The introduction of the musical art also dates from the forty-second year of the same reign, when a musician was brought from the same country.

The art of building was introduced in the sixth year of the reign of the Emperor Jinken (A. D. 488), when carpenters were sent for from Corea.

Thus it is owing to their introduction from China and Corea, that various arts, such as weaving, sewing, building, etc., including medicine and music, were brought to a degree of perfection, although some of these may have originally existed in this country.

In the fourteenth year of the reign of the Emperor Kinmei, he sent orders to Corea to send professors of medicine, divination, and almanac-making, together with books on these arts.

Accordingly, in the year following, a professor of divination, a professor of almanac-making, and professors of medicine, were sent. Besides these, a professor of materia medica and musicians were also sent. They were to stay in this country and hold their offices, to be succeeded by others after a certain length of time, as in the case of the professors of the five classical books.

A priest of Corea, named Kanroku, came in the reign of the Empress Suiko (A. D. 593), and presented books on almanac-making, astronomy, and geography, whereupon students were chosen to be educated in these sciences.

Two students were instructed in almanac-making, one in astronomy, and one in divination, and they all succeeded in their studies. The almanac was first made use of in the beginning of the twelfth year of this reign. The Emperor Tenji made a clepsydra when he was yet a prince, and when he ascended the throne he placed it in a tower built for the purpose, and caused the hours to be struck by means of a bell or a drum, as indicated by the clepsydra. From the above it will be seen that the use of the almanac was introduced from abroad.

Laws being the only effectual means of suppressing crimes and preventing wrongs, are most important provisions for the preservation of peace and order in a country. But in those early times, when people were, notwithstanding a few instances of revolt, so simple and honest that the state of society approximated to that golden age in which general peace and harmony prevailed without any provision to control their action, there existed nothing like distinctly enacted laws. But, in the offices and prayers of religion, there existed petitions which recognized their sins against Heaven and also crimes against their fellow-men, and the ceremonies for their expiation. But when intercourse with foreigners commenced, and the intelligence of the people was consequently more developed, their habits and manners became to some degree also corrupted. Hence, in the twelfth year of the reign of the Empress Suiko (A. D. 604), the Prince Shotoku published seventeen edicts as the laws of the country.

These, however, were nothing more than rules of conduct of a purely instructive nature, and far from what are called laws in modern times. The fact that the main object of legislation was directed to the instruction of the people and the mere prevention of crimes before being committed, shows the kind care taken of the people on the part of the rulers, and the honest and simple manners still preserved on the part of the people in those days. This document of the prince being the oldest of any composed after the style prevalent prior to the Zui and To dynasties in China, is considered by all who have literary taste to belong to the Chinese literary period from 202 B. C. to 264 A. D. These laws of Shotoku are the first official documents in Japan written in the Chinese language.

Origin and Organization of Institutions for Education, Astronomy, Medicine, etc.—The first establishment of a school dates from the reign of the Emperor Tenji (A. D. 668), who in the tenth year of his reign appointed Kishitsu Shushi, a native of Corea, to the office of superintendent of the Educational Department. Previous to this time Yei, a priest of Corea, came to this country and became naturalized. Having the reputation of a great scholar, he was ordered by the emperor to abandon the priesthood, and was appointed superintendent of the Imperial University. Thus originated this educational institution in our country.

An observatory was erected in the fourth year of the reign of the Emperor Tenmu, who was fond of literary pursuits, and especially versed in astronomy and mathematics. The professorship of astronomy was also established, and students were chosen to be educated in this branch of science. In the university, a professorship of the sounds of the Chinese characters and a professorship of penmanship were established, to instruct students who were chosen to study these branches.

The Emperor Monmu extended the educational system by reorganizing the university, provincial schools, a medical department, a musical department, etc., and causing students to be collected into each of these institutions.

The university had one superintendent, one assistant, one professor of the university, two assistant professors, two professors of Chinese sounds, two professors of penmanship, with four hundred students, and one professor of mathematics, with thirty students.

The provincial schools had one professor with fifty students in the great provinces, forty in the first-class provinces, thirty in the middle-class provinces, and twenty in the small provinces.

The medical department had one superintendent, one assistant, one medical professor with forty students, one professor of acupuncture, with twenty pupils, and one professor of shampooing, with ten pupils, one professor of the treatment of diseases of women, and thirty physicians for the same were afterward added. There were attached also to this department a teacher of materia medica, a teacher of cultivating medicinal plants, besides physicians, and persons to practise acupuncture and shampooing.

In each province there was one physician with students whose number was one-fifth of that of the students of the provincial schools.

The astrological department had one superintendent, one assistant, one professor of astrology, one professor of almanac-making, one professor of astronomy, with ten pupils in each of these branches of science, and two professors of chronometry, with twenty keepers of time.

The musical department superintended all matters concerning music. It had one superintendent, one assistant, four singing-masters, thirty singers, one hundred female pupils in singing, and one hundred students of dancing. Besides, there were teachers of the music of China and Corea, each with pupils under his charge. The above is the system which prevailed during the periods A. D. 701-723.

Kiusiu was by far the most important among the provincial governments, having nine provinces and three islands under its jurisdiotion, and exercising the power of imposing taxes, commanding military duty, and dealing with foreign embassadors. In short, it formed an independent government. On this account a special school was established, with a professor of literature, a professor of law, a professor of Chinese sounds, and physicians and keepers of time. The appointment or dismission of professors, as well as the examination of students, was under the sole control of the local government.

In the beginning of the years of Tempiosho-ho (A. D. 749-756), Kibimabi was appointed Lieutenant-Governor of Dazai. He was a man of great learning and did much in spreading literary culture. While he was in his post, he built a school, near the government office, in which he instructed his pupils in the study of literature.

As the Emperor Monmu (A. D. 697) instituted, as already mentioned, the university and provincial schools, a medical department, an astrological department, etc., it became necessary to institute rules and regulations relating to the duties of professors and the tasks of students. Accordingly, regulations for educational institutions were made and distributed.

The regulations for educational institutions, together with such other regulations as are connected with education, will be given in the following pages.

The offices of professor and assistant professor were only to be filled by those whose conduct and knowledge fully qualified them for the position of instructors; and the professorships of penmanship, mathematics, and the sounds of the Chinese characters, were to be occupied by men who were eminently learned in these several arts or sciences, and so also with the professorships of astronomy, medicine, and almanac-making.

The professors of the provincial schools and physicians were to be chosen from among the inhabitants of the respective provinces, and, should proper persons not be found among them, choice was to be made among the inhabitants of neighboring provinces. In case a choice still failed, application for properly-qualified persons was to be made to the Department of Ceremonies, whereupon the vacancies were filled with persons chosen from among the students of the university.

When the governors of provinces and counties were found to be acquainted with the Chinese classics, they were charged with the duty of teaching in conjunction with their own offices.

The pupils of the university were generally chosen from among the children of families not below the fifth rank; but even the children of families down to the eighth rank, if earnestly desiring admission, could obtain the privilege. The pupils of the provincial schools were taken from among those children of governors of counties who were intelligent, and aged from thirteen to sixteen. The grades of students were determined according to their ages, and every student on entering school was required to perform the prescribed ceremony of acknowledging the professors and assistant professors as their teachers. The term of service of professors was to be eight years, and the professors of the provincial schools and physicians were not allowed to retire from their posts until the expiration of the fixed term of service, unless there were sufficient cause for their doing so.

The term of study allowed to pupils was nine years, and those who failed to be taken into the imperial service throughout the term of study were sent home. One day of recreation was allowed to students every ten days; before each recreation-day they were examined by professors in reading-lessons, and those who showed themselves more advanced than the rest in these examinations were admitted to the regular examination made at the end of every year.

In this examination students of the university were examined by the superintendent and assistant superintendent, and those of the provincial schools by the provincial governors. They were divided into first, second, and third classes, according to their abilities displayed in the examination; and those who were put in the lowest class for three successive years were to be dismissed.

The services of the professors and assistant professors were estimated according to their exertions in teaching during one year; thus those under whose instruction pupils made much progress in their study were placed in the highest class. As to the professors of the provincial schools, their services were also estimated by their efforts in instruction, but they were divided into three classes, according to their merits. The services of physicians, too, were estimated according to their success in treating patients.

The books used in teaching were divided into distinct classes:

1.. *The Chinese Classics.*—Shuyeki, or The Art of Divination; Moshi, or The Book of Poems, by Mo; Girai, or The Book of Ceremonies; Kokiyo, or The Book of Filial Affection; Shunju, or The Constitutional History of China; Sho-sho, or The Chinese Imperial Laws; Shu-rai, or The Book of Ceremonies in the Shu dynasty of China; Raiki, or The Book of Ceremonies; Rongo, or The Confucian Analects; Sashiden, or The Comments on Shunju.

To these were subsequently added: Kuyo-Den and Kokurio-Den, or The Comments on Chinese Constitutional History.

2. *The Chinese Historical Works.*—Shiki, or General History; Kan-sho, or The History of the Kan Dynasty; To-kan Kan-ki, or The History of the later Kan Dynasty; Sankoku-Shi, or The History of Three Kingdoms of China; Shin-jo, History of the Shin Dynasty.

3. *Miscellaneous Works.*—Ji-ga, or The Imperial Annals of China; Mon-zen, or Selections from Chinese Literature.

Books on astronomy, medicine, and mathematics, were distributed into their respective classes.

Students were in all cases to study the "Book of Filial Affection" and the "Confucian Analects" besides their principal subjects of study.

In estimating the advancement of the students in learning, certain portions of the above works were considered to be the equivalents of each other, and in making up the grades of the students might be substituted for each other.

The students were not allowed to receive new lessons until they had finished the lessons in the particular classical book which they had commenced to study.

The mode of instruction was first to teach students the sounds of the Chinese characters, and only after they had become thoroughly acquainted with them were they taught to understand the meaning.

Students who had learned to read more than two classical books were allowed to enter into public service. With respect to the students of the provincial schools, if they wished to study more than two classical books, they were transferred to the university.

In both the university and the provincial schools, festivals were observed in honor of Confucius, in the equinoxes of every year. In the university, ceremonies in honor of Confucius and his ten disciples were performed. But in the provincial schools the festivals were celebrated in honor of Confucius and his disciple Ganshi only; but, in the city of Dazai in Kiusiu, one more was added.

The privilege was always given to students of being present at any great ceremonies performed on the occasion of New-Year's day, or festivals. They were also exempt from manual labor of any kind, except on the occasion of festivals observed in honor of Confucius, and of the ceremony performed by students on entering schools. Should students, who left school on account of the death of their parents, apply after the mourning period had expired for readmittance, they were allowed to return to school, provided their age was under twenty-five.

Students were allowed to go home in case either of sickness of themselves or that of their parents, and they were also allowed to be absent from school for fifteen days in the fifth month and in the ninth month of every year. To those whose homes were in distant places, a certain number of days was allowed for traveling. They were not allowed to play music, or make any other merriment in school, except playing on the koto (a stringed musical instrument like the harp), and shooting with bows and arrows. A persistent violation of the prohibition was followed by expulsion from school.

In such cases the reasons of expelling were always to be stated to the proper authority, and then the student was sent to the district to which he belonged.

Although the regulations of educational institutions were thus far completed, the aim was not directed toward the diffusion of knowledge among the people at large, but merely to the education of persons to be employed in the public service. Hence there was a process for selecting students by examination in the Department of Ceremonies.

Students were sent to the examination from the university, and also from the provincial schools. The latter were to be sent to the examination after having been first examined by the provincial governors. Those who obtained the first or second degree in the examination held in the Department of Ceremonies were reported to the emperor, and employed in various offices with different ranks.

Those who obtained the third, or a still lower degree, or who, during the term of their studies, had been dismissed from the university, were not taken into the public service.

The candidates for examination for public service were divided into six classes, according to the branch of study in which they had chiefly engaged, viz.: first, those who had displayed great talents; second, those who had studied not less than two Chinese classics; third, those who had studied political science, and had also learned to read the imperial annals of China and the selections of Chinese literature; fourth, students of law;

fifth, students of penmanship, and, sixth, those in mathematics. To each of these classes only men of integrity and good conduct were admitted.

Different modes were adopted in examining each of these different classes of students. The first were examined in composing two short essays on political questions, and those whose compositions were excellent, both in style and reasoning, stood highest. The second class were examined in reading articles selected from the whole Chinese classics. The third class were examined in composing two propositions on some political question, and in reading selections from the most famous Chinese classics.

The fourth class were examined in articles taken from books on Chinese laws and classics. As to the class of penmanship, facility and elegance of hand were mainly valued, and the style of the characters was not regarded.

The class in mathematics were examined in theorems, selected from Chinese mathematical works. The classes in astronomy, astrology, medicine, and acupuncture, were examined after methods particularly adapted to each of these sciences or arts, as in the case of the university.

Support of Educational Institutions, and Rewards to Professors. —In the first year of Keiun (A. D. 704) an appropriation was made for the support of the university from the public fund reserved for the purpose of meeting incidental expenses.

Again, in the first year of Tenpeihoji (A. D. 757–764), the emperor issued a decree stating that "there is no means better calculated to preserve the safety, peace, and harmony of the people, than the observance of appropriate ceremonies, nor is there any means better adapted to the improvement of the habits of the people than music. . . . This is the reason that etiquette and music have been brought into existence. . . . Now, the students of these important subjects at the university and the musical department should be relieved from the want of the necessaries of life. . . . Astronomy, astrology, almanac-making, mathematics, medicine, and acupuncture, are of no less importance to the country. . . . Therefore the wants of the students of these branches of knowledge should also be provided for by appropriating public lands." Accordingly, thirty chos (one cho being about two and a half acres) were appropriated for the support of the university, and ten chos each for the departments of music, astrology, and medicine.

In the thirteenth year of Yenriyaku (A. D. 794) one hundred and two chos of rice-land in Yechizen were added in consequence of an insufficient supply for the wants of the students of the university, caused by the increase of their number. This, together with the land previously granted, made up one hundred and thirty-two chos of land under the name of "The Educational Land Grant." About the same period Wage Hiroyo, Minister of Education, contributed his property, amounting to twenty chos of land, to the fund of the university.

Subsequently ninety thousand bundles of rice in the sheaf in Hitachi, eighty thousand bundles in Tango, and ten thousand bundles each in Omi, Yechu, Bizen, and Iyo, were loaned to farmers on interest under the superintendence of the provincial governors, and interest in rice was collected. This interest was applied to the payment of miscellaneous expenses of the university.

Another source of school funds was provided by loaning to the inhabitants of the capital new coins, whenever they were made, and appropriating the interest on the loan for the support of students. In the first year of Tencho (A. D. 824) five chos of land in Yamashiro, in the fourth year fifty chos of land in Kawachi, and in the seventh year thirty-seven chos of uncultivated land, and twenty chos of unappropriated land in Omi, were granted to meet the expenditures of students.

From these facts we may form an idea of the large establishment of the university, and the great number of students educated in it at this period.

Public lands were also granted to the departments of astrology and medicine, to support the students, as in the case of the university. In the third year of Tencho, twenty chos of unappropriated land in Kawachi were granted to the astrological department; in the fourth year of "Showa," a piece of ground in the northern part of Kioto was granted to the medical department; in the sixth year a piece of ground formerly belonging to the eastern "Korokan," or the edifice for the reception of foreigners, was converted into an imperial garden for the cultivation of medicinal plants; and in the fifth year of Jokan an unappropriated piece of land in Kawachi was added to the astrological department.

Though such was the patronage given to the several educational establishments by granting lands for their support from age to age, the donations came, in the long course of time, to be improperly managed, and not a small portion of uncultivated and unappropriated lands was neglected to be cultivated, or entirely wasted by floods. So also in the management of the interest on the loans in rice and new coins, many abuses arose, as the officials in charge were from time to time changed, and the inhabitants of the capital came to fail in the payment of the interest on the loans of new coins.

In the eighth year of Genkei (884 A. D.) twenty-three kans of new coins were loaned to the inhabitants of the capital, the interest to be employed in support of the university, in compliance with the request of Fujiwara Sukeyo, the superintendent. Notwithstanding all this, the educational grant was at length transferred to defray the expenses of repairing roads, and other lands were also distributed to other departments, leaving the university, once so flourishing, to almost entire ruin. It is seen in "Daigakushiki," the book containing the regulations of the university, that these funds were, however, restored in consequence of the request made by the assistant minister of the Department of Ceremonies, who stated the evils to the emperor in the fourteenth year of Yengi (A. D. 914).

The practice of granting allowances to students, to enable them to engage exclusively in study, originated in the reign of the Emperor Kanmu (A. D. 782), who was very fond of learning, and who, while yet a prince, himself filled the office of superintendent of the university. On his ascending the throne, he appointed Sugawara Furuhito his tutor, requesting him always to attend him, and treating him with the respect due to a teacher. After the death of Sugawara, the emperor, remembering his former services, and regretting that his four sons were prevented by their poverty from pursuing their hereditary profession, granted them an allowance for the necessaries of life in the fourth year of Yenryaku, and thus enabled them to pursue their studies. This is the first instance in which an allowance for monthly expenses for study was granted.

More than fifty years prior to this period, however, in the second year of Tenpio (A. D. 630), as some historians say, a proposition was made to the emperor and the imperial council, in which was the following passage : " Though the students have passed some length of time in the university, they are still unable to make much progress, and their learning is but superficial, owing to the fact that, although there are persons fond of study, yet they are prevented from accomplishing their object by being destitute of the means of support. . . . Therefore, it is requested that the necessaries of life should be granted to those who are intelligent and much advanced in study, to enable them to engage exclusively in study. . . . It is desirable that the students in the departments of astrology, medicine, and almanac-making, should also be supported, as these branches of knowledge are likewise important and indispensable to the country; while the professors of these sciences are now declining in age, the sciences may be lost forever if they be not studied and transmitted to posterity." The request was sanctioned by the emperor.

This is what is mentioned in some histories, but as it seems that the educational land grant was not yet appropriated at this period, and students were to get their supplies from their own homes, the origin of the practice of supplying students with necessaries is to be dated from the reign of the Emperor Kanmu, instead of this early period.

Since that time, the Sugawara and Oye families both adopted literature as their hereditary profession, expenses for study being always granted to their descendants. An instance of the Suguwara family making application for expenses for study is found in the tenth year of Tenreki (A. D. 956), when Sugawara Fumitoki applied for the allowance for his son Tadahiro in the following words : " This grant originated in my family, it being made to my forefather Kiyogimi, and his three brothers, at the same time. . . . To assist one to succeed to his forefathers' profession is the boundless benevolence of a great patron of literature, and to study and transmit the literary profession of one's ancestors is the duty of the children of the family. . . . For this consideration it is most humbly requested that, by the great favor of the emperor, the monthly allowance be granted to my son to assist him in pursuing his hereditary profession."

In the second year of Koho, he again applied for an allowance to meet the expenses for study of his second son.

We also find the Oye family applying for the grant in the fourth year of Choho, when Oye Masahira made the following request in applying for the expenses of study for his son Yoshigimi, to enable him to succeed to the hereditary profession in the sixth generation: "In consideration of the services of the Sugawara and Oye families in founding a college of literature, to which students constantly resorted for many years for instruction in literature, the children of the two families enjoyed the privilege of being taken into the imperial service, without regard to their abilities and ages, so that Sugawara Tamenori was appointed to office in the seventh generation from his ancestor; and though Taka-oka Sukeyuki, Kamo Yasutaka, etc., were men of high talents and acquirements, they made no opposition to his appointment; and so also with the appointment of Oye Sadamoto, which was never disputed by the most learned men of the age, such as Taguchi Tokina and Yuge Koretoki, who were skilled in prose composition. . . . Such being the honor done to the hereditary profession, it is humbly requested that the expenses for study be granted to my son Yoshigimi, to enable him to succeed early to the hereditary profession."

In the fourth year of the reign of the Empress Jito (A. D. 693) a reward of one thousand bundles of rice in the sheaf was given to Kamikudara, the professor of the university, for the encouragement of literary learning, and twenty rios of silver were given as a reward to each of the professors of Chinese sounds and of penmanship. In the following year a grant of land was made to Kamikudara, and in the seventh year a salary in land, amounting to thirty ko's (land-measure formerly used) was again granted to him. The practice of granting rewards to professional men originated at this period.

In the fourth year of Keiun (A. D. 707), cloth, hoes, salt, and iron, were given to Yamada Mikata. In the first year of Reiki (A. D. 715), Kino Kiyohito, and several others, were each rewarded with ten thousand kokus of rice. In the first year of Yoro (A. D. 717), ten thousand kokus of rice were again given to Kiyohito, and some rewards were also given to other professional men. In the fifth year of Yoro (A. D. 721), an imperial decree was issued that, "as men of the literary profession as well as military men are of great importance to the state, and medicine and mathematics are also cherished in all ages, persons who are qualified as instructors, being learned in literature or science, should be selected and honored with rewards so as to stimulate young scholars." Accordingly, the professors of the university, astronomers, astrologers, physicians, and mathematicians, numbering twenty-eight persons, were rewarded in different proportions. In the following year a quantity of rice-land was distributed among twenty-three persons as a reward.

During the period of Tenpeihoji (A. D. 757), it was decreed that professors of the provincial schools, and physicians, when first appointed to their offices, should each send one year's income to their former teachers as a token of gratitude; whereby the respect due to teachers would be kept up, and the work of instruction continually performed. In the fifth year of Showa (A. D. 838), an imperial decree was issued that, "according to the established regulations, professors and physicians in every province are each to send one year's income to their former teachers from the time of their appointments; but, complaint being apt to arise when a whole year's salary is exacted, a proper rate is therefore to be fixed for them in proportion to the size of the provinces: two hundred bundles of rice in the straw in the first-class provinces, and fifty bundles in the lowest-class provinces, should be made the fixed rate, and these should be sent, after being exchanged for articles of a light kind of the products of the respective provinces. . . . Those sent from professors should be sent to the university, and those from physicians to the medical department." In the twelfth year of Jokan, a modification was made in this regulation, and one-tenth of the amount of income was made the fixed rate. This was made the permanent rule, being embodied in the regulations established during the years of Yengi.

Regulations of the University.—The subjects of instruction in the university were divided into the following departments:

1. KIDEN.—The principal subject of study being history, and the art of composition.

2. MEIKEI.—The principal subject of study being the six Chinese classical books and the annotated editions of the constitutional history of China.

3. MEIHO.—In this department books on penal law, and the books of the imperial edicts, together with the books of rules and regulations for officials, were principally studied.

4. SANDO.—In this department arithmetic and mathematics were exclusively studied.

When the imperial mandates were codified during the years of Taiho (A. D. 701-703), a professorship was established under the title of Dai-hakase, or great professor, and this professor had duties both in the departments of history and the Chinese classics. Subsequently these departments were divided each into separate subjects of instruction, by increasing the number of professorships.

The following list of professors is mentioned in a document concerning the rewards given to professional men in the fifth year of Yoro (A. D. 721), viz.:

First-class professors in the Chinese classics: Kanuchi Osumi, and Ochi-hiroyo.

Second-class professors in the same branch: Sena Yukibumi, Tsuki Furumaro, Nukata Chitari.

Professors of law: Yazu Mushimaro, Shi-oya Yoshimaro.

Professors of the art of composition: Yamada Mikata, Shimotsuke Mushimaro, Kino Kiyohito, and Sazanami Kawachi.

Professors of mathematics: Yamaguchi Tanushi, Shikino Mitatsuki, and Kisakibe Iwamura.

Professors of astrology: Otsu Opito, Tsumori Michigimo, Nakabumi Yemaro, Yoshin-shoshe, and Shigabe Amida.

Professors of medicine: Kitusen, Goshiku, Komei, Taichogen, and Yega Kunishige.

The department of historical study and the art of composition being considered from an early period the most difficult one, it was assigned to the first place. The department of law was established for studying laws and jurisprudence, and Mushimaro and Furumaro were appointed professors of this branch, to arrange laws and edicts. Besides, there were professors of the sounds of the Chinese characters, and of penmanship, who instructed pupils in these respective branches.

Every student was at first instructed to read the classical books with the correct sounds of the Chinese characters, under the instruction of the professor; there was therefore no separate class of students for the study of that art; and so also with penmanship. But at a subsequent period those students who exclusively engaged in studying the sounds of the Chinese characters and penmanship came to form each a distinct class, under the titles of "students of the sounds of letters" and "students of penmanship." Yenshin, a native of To (China), being well versed in the sounds of the Chinese characters, was appointed by the imperial orders professor of the art. In the seventh year of Tenpio (A. D. 735) every student was ordered to study the sounds under his instruction.

As characters were first introduced from Corea, the Go-On (corrupt sound used probably by the natives of the eastern part of China) was mostly used instead of Kuan-On (pure sound), both in speaking and reading.

In a work about the island Tsushima, it is mentioned that there lived a nun in the island who taught the inhabitants the sacred books of Buddhism in the Go-On; and consequently these sounds came to be exclusively used in reading the Chinese classical books; hence originated the name Tsushima-On, or the sounds used by the inhabitants of Tsushima. This is the reason that the professorship of the pure sounds of the Chinese characters was established. Although the rule for pronouncing the Chinese characters was for the first time settled on the return of Kibi-mabi from China, where he had been educated, the use of the corrupt sounds was by no means discontinued. To remedy this evil a decree was issued, by the emperor, to the effect that all the students in the department of Chinese classics should be thoroughly educated in the use of the proper sounds of Chinese. At a later period the rule was fixed that the Kuan-On should be used in reading books of Confucianism, and the Go-On in books of Buddhism only; but in the twelfth year of Yenriyaku an imperial decree was issued prohibiting the admission of any candidate to the priesthood unless he had learned to use the Kuan-On. In the twentieth year it was again decreed that in the annual examination of candidates for the priesthood only those who, being intelligent and respectable in conduct, and also learned in the use of the Kuan-On, were qualified to be priests, or be admitted to the priesthood. Thus it is evident that the Kuan-On was not preferred in reading books of Confucianism only.

In the fifth year of Jinki (A. D. 728) professorships of criminal law and jurisprudence, and also a lectureship, were established. This is the beginning of the professorship of each distinct branch of knowledge being made a permanent office. In the second year of Tenpio students were chosen to be instructed in these branches of knowledge. Those who exclusively engaged in historical study were called historical students, and those engaged in studying the Chinese classics were called classical students. There was a class of students called Tokugiosei (fellows) in each branch of study, with the privilege of being furnished with clothes for all seasons. A certain number of those who were most talented and accomplished in each branch were put into this class. Their term of study was seven years.

In the medical department students were instructed to read the books on medicinal plants, the treatise on the state of pulsation, and the treatises on the human body. The principal subject of the study of medical plants referred to their forms and properties. The anatomy of the human body was studied by examining diagrams. The conditions and movements of the pulse as affected by the temperature of the seasons were learned. The students were also to read different Chinese medical books for two years. After having gone through this course of study they then proceeded to solve the meaning of what they had learned, and to perform practical operations. Medical treatment was divided into several branches—namely, the treatment of diseases of the internal parts of the body; the treatment of incised wounds, ulcers, and all other diseases belonging to external parts of the body; the treatment of the diseases of infants; the treatment of diseases of the ear, eye, mouth, and teeth. Forty students were distributed to these branches, twenty-four being assigned to the study of internal diseases, with a term of study of seven years, of which the first four years were to be applied to initiatory studies, and three more were assigned to diseases of the eye, ear, and mouth. Besides these, there were students of acupuncture, students of shampooing, and physicians of the diseases of women. The students of acupuncture were to study the art by reading and examining the treatise of Kotei on acupuncture, and the diagram of the human skeleton, the term of study of seven years being allowed to them. The students of shampooing were instructed in the art of treating bruises and fractures, and in bandaging wounds, three years being their term of study. The physicians of the diseases of women were instructed to assist women in childbirth, and also to treat incised wounds, ulcers, and bruises. They were also to study the practice of acupuncture and of applying moxa. In studying these arts they were not required to read books treating of them, but merely to learn the practical operations. Accordingly, the professor of diseases of women taught the students only by giving them lessons orally from books. The term of study of this class was seven years.

The same ceremonies for admission were required, and the same privileges allowed to these students as to the students of the university.

The students of medicine and acupuncture were to be chosen first from among the children of the families who belonged hereditarily to the medical profession, and next from among the children of the people at large. Children who were intelligent and aged between thirteen and sixteen were to be chosen. As to the physicians of the diseases of women, those who were intelligent and aged from fifteen to twenty-five were chosen from among the maids of the court, and they were, when chosen, placed in a separate building.

The students of literature were examined once a month by the professors, once a season by the superintendent or assistant superintendent of the university, and at the end of the year they were examined by the Department of the Imperial Household. The physicians of diseases of women were examined by the court physicians, and the mode of examination was precisely the same as that in use at the university. Those who had failed in the examination in theoretical learning, but who manifested practical abilities, and were able to treat diseases, were allowed to practise acupuncture. Any person who studied and practised the medical art was allowed to enter and undergo an examination in the same manner as the regular students. The number of " fellows " in the medical department was three in the second year of Tenpio; but in the fifth year of Konin the number was increased to four, and the same supply of provisions and clothes and the same term of study were allowed to them as those in the university. This increase was in consequence of a proposition then made that "medicine and acupuncture are of great importance to the country, while it is feared that these arts should decline and professors of the arts might become extinct at length, if their study be not encouraged."

The tasks and term of study of medical students in the provincial schools were the same as those of the medical department in the capital. They were examined by physicians of the provinces once a month, and at the end of every year they were examined by the provincial governors, who fixed their grades according to their abilities. Those students who were much advanced, if they desired to be employed, were reported to the Imperial Council, as to their abilities, by the provincial governors, and were taken into the imperial service.

In the department of astronomy, the relative position of the sun and moon, the five planets, and the twenty-eight constellations, and various phenomena of the atmosphere, were observed, in order to foretell the good or evil fortunes likely to occur during the year. The astronomical portions of Chinese history were studied.

In the astrological department future events were divined, and modes of avoiding evil influences were determined. The Chinese books of divination, etc., were the text-books.

In the branch of almanac-making, calculations of the motion of the sun, moon, and stars, were made, and the number of days and months, etc., in the year, was published.

The text-books were the astronomical portions of Chinese histories. Students were chosen first from among the children of the families hereditarily professing divination, and then from among the children of the people at large, in the same manner as medical students. Their tasks, term of study, and ages, were fixed by the same rule as that in the university. The fixed number of "fellows" was three in the astrological department, and two in the department of almanac-making, their privileges, etc., being the same as those in the university.

There were provided celestial globes and other astronomical instruments for the use of the students. There was a distinct class of students under the title of "observers," who were always to observe the aspects of the heavens and watch the various phenomena of the atmosphere, not being permitted to read books of any sort. Their term of study was not fixed, and the same supply of provisions and clothes as was allowed to "fellows" was granted to them.

The almanac was always to be prepared in advance by computing the times beforehand, and to be presented to the emperor by the first day of the eleventh month. One copy was sent to every official in such a manner as to reach him within the year.

It was in the twelfth year of the reign of the Empress Suiko (A. D. 604) that the almanac was first used. The almanac then used was that of the Zui dynasty, in China, introduced by a priest of Corea. It being at a later period found to be incorrect, another almanac was adopted in the sixth year of the reign of the Empress Jito (A. D. 695). After being used for five years, this almanac was found to be behind the true time by fifty-three kokus (a koku being one hundredth of twenty-four hours). Consequently, in the first year of the reign of the Emperor Monmu a new almanac was adopted and used for sixty-seven years, till the eighth year of Tempeihoji, when it was found to be behind the true time by fourteen kokus, and was replaced by the almanac which had been presented to the emperor by Kibimabi. This being found in the course of fourteen years to be ahead of the true time by seventeen kokus, another almanac was adopted in the second year of Ten-an, which was also found after only four years' time to be behind the true time by ten kokus. In the fourth year of Jokan, another new almanac was adopted, and continued to be in use for eight hundred and twenty-three years without being altered. These almanacs were brought from China under the Zui and To dynasties, and none was originally composed in this country.

In the second year of Jokio a student of astronomy named Yasui Santetsu, a native of Yedo, corrected, by permission of the Government, the almanac then in use, on account of its being behind the true time by one hundred and ninety-five kokus. This, again, in the course of seventy years, came to be ahead of the true time by seven kokus. Therefore a new almanac was made by making new calculations of time in the fifth year of Horeki. After the lapse of forty-three years it fell behind the true time by four kokus. So in the tenth year of Kuansei another almanac was adopted, but after a time, a slight error being found in it, a new one was adopted in the fourteenth year of Tenpo (A. D. 1843), and was used until the adoption of the solar year instead of the lunar one used heretofore, which took place in the fifth year of Meiji (A. D. 1872). The time contained in the year was then for the first time made to correspond to the true time.

Regulations of Provincial Schools.—Though the educational institutions in the provinces were founded on the same system as that of the university, the medical department, the astrological department, etc., they were found defective, arising from the inability of the teachers. To remedy the evil, an imperial decree was issued in the second year of Keiki, that the professorships of the provincial schools should not be filled by those students of the university who used to hunt for office while they were yet imperfectly learned. Notwithstanding, this office continued to be hunted by persons unqualified for the station, and consequently many were found among the teachers who were not yet sufficiently learned. This led to the issue of another imperial decree, proclaimed in the first year of Tenpeihoji (A. D. 757), to the effect that "many of the professors and physicians in the several provinces are found to have obtained their offices, not by virtue of their abilities, but merely by begging them. . . . This, being not only an impediment to the administration of government, but also a disadvantage to the people, should be put an end to. . . . Students hereafter will not be admitted into the public service unless they have learned all the books required to be studied in their respective offices. . . . The students of the Chinese classics should have studied the five classical books; the students of history the three histories; the students of medicine, astronomy, etc., each must have studied the works prescribed for his course."

The above was the established rule for selecting and appointing the students of the university to the offices of professors and physicians in the provinces, but many of the books above mentioned were not provided in the provincial schools.

Thus in the third year of Jingo-keiun (A. D. 769) an application was made by the city of Dazai for the supply of the three histories, stating that "the city of Dazai, being one of the largest cities in the country, and its population being so dense, the number of students is constantly increasing, while books supplied for their use consist only of the five classical books, while the three histories are not as yet provided. . . . Therefore, it is requested that one copy of the three histories be supplied in order to give encouragement to education within the jurisdiction of the Dazai Government." In compliance with the request one copy each of the three histories of Go, Gi, and Shoku, or the history of Shin, was ordered by the emperor to be supplied to the city of Dazai. Subsequently imperial orders were given to the provinces of Sagami, Musashi, Hitachi, Kotsuke, Shimotsuke, and Mutsu, to make copies of the three histories and to send them to the Government. These facts show the scarcity of books in those days.

In the eleventh year of Tenpio (A. D. 739) the children of noble families above the fifth rank in the Department of Ceremonies were ordered to be admitted to the university without distinction as to their ages. According to the old rule established during the years of Taiho, the choice of students was limited to the children of families above the fifth rank, and to those of families not below the eighth rank, who particularly desired to be admitted, and to those of the hereditary literary families, and their ages were limited from thirteen to sixteen, in all branches of knowledge. Now that the limit of admittance was extended, the number of students became greatly increased, so that the Empress Koken appropriated some lands for the support of the students, under the title of the "Educational Land-Grant."

In the eighth year of Yenriyaki (A. D. 789) regulations were established by which appointments of students of the university to any office should not take place under the age of thirty. In the thirteenth year a large extent of land was appropriated to meet the expenses of the university. In the first year of Daido all the royal princes and the children of families above the fifth rank who were above ten years of age were made to enter the university to be educated in the various branches of knowledge assigned to them, but, owing to the diversity of character of students, and the consequently various propensities possessed by them for particular pursuits, many were found to be unable to succeed even in a single branch of knowledge after having passed many years in study. On this account an arrangement was made by an imperial decree issued for that purpose in the first year of Tencho, by which they were allowed to choose themselves those pursuits which they thought most suited to their tastes and propensities. After thirteen years from this period a petition was sent to the emperor from the university, stating that, "on account of the edict which has long been in operation, excluding students under thirty years of age from employment, there are found many who, though most earnestly devoted to Confucianism and most diligently applying themselves to study, still are suffering from poverty, not being allowed to be employed for many years after having accomplished their study. . . . There seems no reason why age should be taken into consideration when talent is the main question, and it is requested that the students be admitted into Government service on examination as to their abilities according to the former rules."

The request was sanctioned by the emperor.

All young persons aged over twenty, belonging to families above the fifth rank, were ordered to enter the university to be educated to read classical and historical works, and those who made such progress as to be fit to be employed were appointed to different offices according to their abilities. This arrangement was made in consequence of the young men of noble families coming gradually to indulge themselves in luxury and license, instead of applying themselves to study. At a later period, great families, such as Fujiwara and Tachibana, established private schools for the education of young persons belonging to their respective families. When the students of law and literature were first chosen in the second year of Tenpio, their fixed numbers were ten and twenty in those two classes respectively. In the twenty-first year the number of students of the former class was increased to twenty; and in the fourth year of Konin, in consideration of more difficulty attending the study of the law-class than any other kind of study, and with the view of giving encouragement to those students who, it was found, might be wearied out and prevented from finishing their study on account of the difficulty of their tasks, a change was introduced in the regulations for examination, by which the old rule of admitting into public service only those who gave satisfactory answers to eight points or more out of ten proposed in the examination, and excluding all those who could not give answers to more than seven points, was replaced by a new rule of appointing all those who were able to give answers on more than seven points to the professors of the provincial schools. In choosing the students of the literature-class, all intelligent children of the gentry might be chosen, not limiting their ages; but, in the twelfth year of Konin, a regulation was established prohibiting the selection of children of any other families than those above the third rank. Those moderately advanced in study, among the students, were to form a class called "Shunshi" (literally, men of talent), and the most intelligent of this class were distinguished under the title of "Shusai" (literally, men of rare talent). This regulation for examination remained unaltered; hence the admittance to the Shusai class, and the study of the art of composition, were limited to the children of noble families, to the exclusion of all other students.

In the fourth year of Tencho (A. D. 827), Miyako Haraka, the professor of the art of composition, requested the emperor to alter the rule for choosing students, stating that "it is feared that scholars of the art of composition may cease to be produced, if this branch of study be, as it now is, limited to men of high birth only, since men of noble birth cannot be expected always to be men of talent, nor are men of great talent necessarily of noble birth. Still more, the university is a place where talent ought to be cherished and intelligence nourished; and, besides, what the scholars consider their hope and honor is, that talent alone is cared for by rulers in choosing men, so that one who is a mere common domestic in the morning may be raised to the station of minister of state in the evening. For these reasons it is humbly requested that students should be permitted to be chosen according to the regulation established in the second year of Tenpio."

In former times, whenever embassadors were sent to the courts of the Zui or To dynasty (China), scholars who possessed intellect and knowledge were selected to follow them. Takamuku Kuromasa, etc., were the first students sent to China in the reign of the Empress Suiko (A. D. 593–628), and after that time students were often sent.

In the second year of Reiki (A. D. 716), Abe Nakamaro and Kibimabi were chosen as students to be sent to China, and they studied the Chinese classics and other branches of learning with success, and obtained great reputation for their knowledge in that country, The latter returned in the seventh year of Tenpio, after having remained in China for eighteen years, and presented to the emperor books treating on the etiquette of the To dynasty and almanac-making. He was appointed assistant superintendent of the university.

The ceremonies to be performed at the festival of Confucius were settled by his dictation, and all the instruments to be used on the occasion were also completed under his superintendence; thus the forms and etiquette came for the first time to be performed with propriety. He was honored with the appointment of Udaijin (one of the highest officers in the government), and died in the sixth year of Hoki. Nakamaro adopted the name of Choko and died in China, having been in the service of the court of that country for more than fifty years.

After a while, in the latter part of the period Yenriyaku, Tachibana Hayanari was sent to China as a student, and was respected as the "talented Tachibana."

Embassadors to the court of the To dynasty ceased to be sent in the seventh year of Kanpio, on account of the fall of that dynasty. Consequently the sending of students to China was also discontinued.

Educational Institutions and Libraries at Kioto.—The Emperor Kanmu (A. D. 782–805) founded the imperial castle, in Yamashiro, which he made the seat of government, divided the city now known as Kioto into two parts, constructed streets, and built edifices for various departments of government. He also established the university with capacious school-rooms and abodes for students, in a locality in the southern portion. He also instituted medical and astrological departments, with professors and students in each. These institutions were full of students, and enjoyed a notable degree of prosperity.

During the reign of the Emperors Saga, Junna, Ninmio, and Montoku (A. D. 810–858), education received constant attention, and a large number of men of great talent and learning was produced. However, after the middle ages the literary profession became an hereditary calling and was pursued by certain families, and the offices of superintendent, assistant superintendent, and professors in the university, medical and astrological departments, were not by the established rule to be filled by other than the persons belonging to these privileged families. Thus the art of composition and the study of history were the exclusive profession of the Sugawara and Oye families; the study of law, that of the Sakano-uye and Nakahara families. The offices of judge, and of policeman, were also to be held by these two families; the study of mathematics belonged to the Mi-yoshi and Kotsuki families, and medicine to the Wage and Niwa families. Astrology was formerly professed only by the Kamo family, but, in the year of Tenyen (A. D. 973-975), Kamo Yasunori instructed his son Mitsuyoshi in almanac-making, and his pupil Abe Seimei in astronomy; hence the profession of astrology became divided between the two families. The hereditary profession was most successfully kept up in the Sugawara family, from which men of great talent and learning successively sprung up and instructed their pupils in the school which had been built by the family. This is the first private school ever founded in this country, and was followed by other schools of like character.

The school founded by Sugawara, the professor of the art of composition, in the latter part of the period of Konin (A. D. 823), consisted of two buildings constructed in the compound of the university, to accommodate the students of the art of composition and history.

In the early period of Showa the school was placed under the divided superintendence of Oye Otohito and Sugawara Kiyogimi; the former superintending the eastern building, and the latter the western. All young men of different families who wanted public employment flocked to these two families to receive instruction, so that this school was the most populous one of the time.

A school was founded by Fujiwara Fuyutsugu in the second year of Tencho. He built the school for the purpose of educating the youth of his family, which had greatly increased, and appropriated a piece of land measuring one thousand ko's for the support of the school. He also purchased a certain extent of rice-land for the same purpose. This school, being located in the southern direction of the university, was called the southern hall, in distinction from the eastern and western halls. Fuyutsugu also founded a charity-hospital, to receive and maintain poor persons of his family. After his death the income from the land appropriated for the support of the school became insufficient to meet expenses. His son Yoshifusa, regretting the decline of the school, made an application to the emperor, in conjunction with Morotsugu, a member of the same family, for an endowment to the school, in the period Showa (A. D. 834-847). Their request was granted, and the school was restored to its former condition. Subsequently a superintendent and a chief instructor were appointed in the institution, and a ceremony of annually presenting its graduates to the public service was also introduced.

In the third year of Kisho (A. D. 850) a school was founded by the consort of the Emperor Saga, who had undertaken, in conjunction with her brother, Ujigimi, to build a school in which young persons of her family—namely, that of Tachibana—might be educated in the Chinese classics and histories. Notwithstanding the death of her brother, she executed her design in establishing the school, and appropriated some land for its support. In the first year of Koko this institution was made a branch of the university by the imperial order.

Junnain was formerly a pleasure-house of the Emperor Junna (A. D. 824-833), and was called the Western Palace. After the death of the emperor, his son, the Prince Tsunesada, having asked the permission of the emperor then reigning, converted the palace into a school, and appointed a superintendent for the education of all young persons of the O family.

A school was founded by Ariwara Yukihira, the son of the Prince Awo, and the grandson of the Emperor Nara, in the fifth year of Genkei (A. D. 831), and was made the southern hall of the university, it being situated on the western side of the school of Fujiwara, and on the southern side of the university adjoining it. It had been intended for the students of the O family to study penmanship. The term O was adopted as a family name by all those who descended from the royal princes in three or four generations, and still had no particular family name given them by the emperor. As to Yukihira, he had this particular family name given him by the emperor; therefore it seems that he established this school for the children of his relations. In the third year of Oho this school was in all respects assimilated to that of Fujiwara. Subsequently it was transferred to the superintendence of the Minamoto family, who, being also the descendants of the Emperors Saga, Murakami, and Seiwa, were entitled to superintend the school according to the established rule.

Though the above four schools were originally founded on private account, at length being resorted to by a great number of scholars of all families, they were assimilated to the public institutions, and had a larger number of students than the university.

As to libraries, there is no mention made of any considerable one being established in all these ages. During the period Hoki (A. D. 770–780) a person named Ishigami Iyetsugu converted his residence into a temple, and within the grounds of the temple built a house, in which he stored books, and allowed any one to read the books at pleasure. This is the first instance mentioned of collecting books for public use. In the early part of the period of Yenriyaku (A. D. 782–806), Wagekiyomaro, the Minister of the Interior, undertook to provide a library in his own residence for the use of his family, but did not attain his object. Hiroyo, his son, executed his father's intention in providing a building, in which he kept several thousands of books, and appropriating forty cho's of land to meet expenses for keeping up the establishment. This was the largest library of the times. At a later period the Sugawara family had accumulated and possessed books from generation to generation, and when the famous Michizane succeeded to the family title he built a study in his new residence at Gojo, in which he stored the books. In the centre of this study was a storehouse for the reception of books, which were kept in small cases, and arranged upon three shelves placed one above another, on four sides of the house. It is mentioned in his own memoir, written in the fifth year of Kanpei (A. D. 893), that the study came to be called Rinmon by the scholars on account of there having been nearly one hundred students educated in this study who had been taken into public employment. The Oye family kept up its hereditary profession for eight generations, and consequently accumulated a large number of books during three hundred years. Oye Masafusa built a library at Takahura in Nijo. Some one remarked to him that, as fires were so frequent in the capital, he should take it into consideration in regard to his books. To this he replied that the fate of his hereditary profession of literature depended upon that of the Imperial Government.

and, as long as the Government was in a flourishing state, there was nothing to be feared about the safety of the books. When the books were destroyed by fire in the period of Ninpei (A. D. 1051–1053), the Imperial Government was also in a declining state, and it was said by all that he had a correct foresight.

At a later period a library was built by Fujiwara Yorimasa, the Sadaijin, who, being fond of literary pursuits, engaged in the study of the Chinese classics, and purchased many books. The interior of the library was furnished with shelves on the eastern and western sides, upon which books were placed, being divided into the four classes of classics, histories, miscellaneous, and Japanese books. The greater part of these consisted of books he himself had copied. A merchant of the kingdom of the So dynasty, hearing of the library, contributed to it "The History of the To Dynasty" and the history of the five kingdoms of China.

During three hundred and eighty years from the period of Hokio (A. D. 770) to this time there were no more than these few instances to be mentioned of libraries, and, after one hundred and fifty years had again passed, Kanazawa Bunko, or the library of Kanazawa, was built by Kanazawa Akitoki; and, after the lapse of another fifty years, books possessed by Uyesugi Norezane were collected and stored in the school of the Ashigaga family. It is, indeed, by these two families last mentioned that literary learning amid wars and disturbances narrowly escaped its extinction, and was transmitted to posterity.

The account of the restoration of learning, which was brought to the brink of extinction during the periods Keicho and Genna, will be given in the next chapter.

CHAPTER III.

EDUCATION UNDER THE SHOGUNATE.

By the rigor of military discipline disorder in a country is suppressed, but peace is not preserved without literary knowledge. This truth was not unknown to our former emperors, for in the observance of it they, in ancient times, when in a flourishing condition, directed their attention to literature as well as military affairs. They established at Kioto and in the several provinces garrisons for the preservation of order. At the same time, in Kiushi, a local government was established at Dazai to keep out the Western barbarians; and in Mutzu a military government was established to keep the Eastern barbarians in subjection. They founded in Kioto an Imperial University; and in the provinces of the empire provincial schools were opened. They also made many laws and regulations under which learning and science flourished.

In religion the majority of all classes professed the doctrines of Buddhism, so that even the emperors were satisfied to rank themselves among its believers. Still Confucianism was by no means neglected, but was studied as before. The educational system established and supported by the Government exerted a good influence on the morals and manners of the people, and helped to train up virtuous men and women. In the first year of the period Tempei-hoji (A. D. 757), the Empress Koken issued an edict to the following effect: "Filial piety is the foundation on which to govern the state and to preserve public peace, and, as there is nothing more important than this, every house should preserve a copy of the Chinese book on 'Filial Piety,' and it should be read night and day." This plan was copied from the Chinese. It was at this time that education began to be diffused by the Government among the masses of the people. Following this was a period when the imperial power was usurped by the military subjects, for several hundred years, and the educational system could not be kept in so flourishing a condition as in former times, and it was not until the time when Tokugawa Iyeyasu rose into power as shogun, or military chief under the emperor, that scholars were esteemed, Confucianism respected, the art of government studied, and the benefit of education began to spread itself once more over the empire.

Literary Institutions.—In the sixth year of Keicho (A. D. 1601), Iyeyasu founded for the first time a school at Fushimi, near Kioto, in Yamashiro, for the purpose of encouraging literature.

After he had gained the battle of Seki-ga-hara, where he finally crushed the power of his enemies, he became the actual, though not the titular, ruler of the whole empire of Japan. He encouraged literature and education. In the nineteenth year of Keicho (A. D. 1614), at the request of Doshun, he founded another school at Kioto, and chose Seikuwa as its chief.

Seikuwa was a son of the Councilor Tamezumi, and had joined in his youth the Buddhist priesthood, which, however, he afterward renounced, and began to give lectures on the Chinese classics at Kioto, upon which the priests of Gozan rose in opposition to him, urging that, in accordance with the custom established since the Ashikaga dynasty, no one could collect students and deliver lectures to them except their order alone. It will be seen from this incident how low education had fallen at this time.

Seikuwa, far from being discouraged by this opposition, undertook the restoration of moral education to its former state.

His disciples gradually increased, and his fame spread abroad. Many imperial nobles and territorial princes became his followers, and such great scholars as Hayashi Doshun, Matzunaga Shosan, Nawa Kuwasshio, Kuwan Gendo, Ishikawa Jozan, Hori Kio-an, and others, were educated under him. Iyeyasu, hearing of his fame, called him, in the second year of Bunroku (A. D. 1593), to Yedo, and ordered him to deliver lectures on the " Book of Political Science."

Afterward he begged leave to retire, and returned to Kioto, where he was made the head of a school. It was his desire to build halls for the use of students, which he proposed to get endowed with land, and also to assemble all the illustrious and wise men of his time, so that he might consult them on matters of school administration. But at this time the battle of Osaka was fought, and soon after Iyeyasu died; he was, therefore, unable to carry out his project. In the fifth year of Genna (A. D. 1619) he died, in the fifty-ninth year of his age.

To him we are indebted for the revival of literature and the restoration of education. The former system of education had been pulled to the ground during the perpetual wars which raged in the latter part of the Ashikaga Government, and he devoted himself entirely to its restoration.

It was in the seventh year of Kuwanye (A. D. 1630) that Tokugawa Hidetada bestowed on Hayashi Doshun a piece of land at Uyeno, in Yedo, for his residence, and here Doshun founded a private school.

On part of this ground Yoshinobu, Prince of Owari, in the tenth year of Kuwanye (A. D. 1633), caused a temple to be erected in honor of Confucius, which he called the Sage's Temple; here ceremonies were performed in honor of Confucius, in the middle months of spring and autumn. Upon this, for the first time, reverence and esteem began to be entertained by all classes for Confucian learning.

The Hayashi family, from the time of Doshun, continued successively to superintend school affairs under the Tokugawa family. Doshun's son was Jo, and his grandson, Ko; they both added to the fame of the family name, and at length this family held supreme power in all literary matters of the empire.

Hayashi Doshun was born at Kioto. While yet a child he studied at the monastery Kenninji of Higashiyama, and even at this early age his literary talents were so great that the priests of the monastery bore him much affection; they tried to prevail upon him to enter upon a religious life, but he did not follow their advice. Afterward he was taught by Fujiwara Seikuwa, and he became a believer in the teachings of Chinese philosophy.

In his twentieth year he began to assemble students, and commenced to deliver lectures on the "Confucian Analects." In those days, according to the old established custom, all the professors of the classics at the imperial court made use of the old commentaries to interpret the Chinese classics; but now Doshun alone commenced to teach the new Chinese philosophy. Upon this Kiyowara Hidekata, one of the professors, denounced him, and petitioned that he might be punished; for, being a private individual, it was alleged that he had, without being in a position which entitled him to do so, delivered lectures on the Chinese classics, and, moreover, he had done so without adhering to the old commentaries. Iyeyasu, however, rejecting the petition, bestowed his favor on Doshun, and made him his adviser. Later on Doshun shaved his head, and received a sacerdotal title. He reëstablished the ceremonies of the imperial court upon their ancient footing, and revised the laws and edicts. Indeed, at this time there was no proclamation or government document issued which did not pass through his hands. He served in succession four shoguns, and thus, becoming well versed in the old precedents of the court, always took part in the discussions held on the forms and ceremonies to be observed on all such public occasions as the coronation, the change in the name of the year, the processions of the emperor, or the ceremonies to be observed upon admission to the imperial presence, and upon offering sacrifices at the ancestral temple, and on those to be observed in foreign intercourse. He died in the third year of Meireki (A. D. 1657), in the seventy-fifth year of his age, leaving behind him works on one hundred and thirty different subjects, and essays to the number of one hundred and fifty volumes. He was succeeded by his son Jo.

Hayashi Jo, or Shunsai, as he was more commonly called, was the third son of Doshun. In the seventeenth year of his age he accompanied his father to Yedo, and there assisted him in the compilation of his works. He principally devoted himself to the compilation of a genealogical record of noted Japanese families, consisting of more than three hundred volumes, commenced by his father under government orders in the seventeenth year of Kuwanye (A. D. 1640), and completed after twenty years of labor. To Shunsai is mainly due the merit of its composition. In the third year of Manji (A. D. 1660) he repaired, at the expense of the shogun's government, the Confucian temple. In the first year of Kuwanbun (A. D. 1661) he received a promotion to a high priestly rank, and in the third year (A. D. 1663), in honor of his scholastic attainments, he was created a doctor.

About this time, having obtained the government permission, he undertook the completion of a history of Japan, commencing with the reign of the Emperor Jimmu, and carried up to the end of the reign of the Emperor Uda. This work had been left unfinished by his father. For this purpose he established, at the side of the Confucian temple, an historiographer's office, and here he worked at the completion of the above-mentioned history. This work was completed after seven years of labor, during which time he was assisted by his two sons, and by more than thirty assistants of his own training; upon these daily wages and monthly allowances were bestowed by the Government. When this history was about to be published, it was subjected to the revision of the Princes of Owari, Kii, and Mito; and the last of these, Mitsukuni, Prince of Mito, attacked it, and was strongly opposed to its being published, because, he said, it contained singular opinions concerning the Emperor Jimmu. Its publication was on this account stopped. Upon this the historiographer's office was converted into a hall for students, and the fund granted for the compilation of historical works was used for their support.

In the twelfth year of Kuwanbun (A. D. 1672) another hall, on the eastern side of the old one, was erected, with materials supplied by the Government. This was named the Eastern Hall, while the other was called the Western. In the eighth year of Yempo (A. D. 1680), Shunsai died, in the sixty-third year of his age. His son Ko succeeded him.

Hayashi Ko was the second son of Shunsai. He first took as his common name Shun-jo, which he afterward changed for that of Tokushin. At this time Tsunayoshi was shogun; he was very fond of study, and patronized Tokushin, whose house being at a great distance from the castle, the shogun gave him a new residence within the castle-ramparts.

In the fourth year of Teikio (A. D. 1687) he received a sacerdotal title, and also succeeded to his father's title of doctor. In the third year of Genroku (A. D. 1690) he was ordered to remove the Sage's Temple in his grounds to Ushima, where it was rebuilt with great magnificence, and called Tai-sei-den. In the following year the Shogun Tsunayoshi personally visited this temple, and performed the ceremony in honor of the sage ; on this occasion he made this temple a land-endowment, in order to meet the expenditure consequent upon the annual festival held in the sage's honor ; besides which, he also endowed it with a permanent fund for the purpose of supporting a large number of students. Such was the source from which the college of Sho-hei originated ; and, in fact, at no time since the period of Keicho (A. D. 1596–1614) had learning been so prosperous ; for now everybody, from the nobility down to the masses of the people, began to esteem and appreciate literary studies.

Rise of the Literary Profession.—Since the time of the Ashikaga shogunate, wars had raged year after year, and the "samurai," or military class of the people, had devoted themselves entirely to military arts, while the cultivation of literature had long been left entirely in the hands of the Buddhist priests; consequently, great scholars such as Seikuwa and Doshun, although as Confucianists they had raised themselves to high positions, still had been obliged to take the priests for their teachers, to shave their heads, and to assume the appearance of being the followers of Buddhism, receiving sacerdotal titles ; this made them a body distinct from the rest of the samurai and nobility.

Tokushin now complained of the injustice he suffered from this custom, urging that, as Confucianism was the code of principles to be observed by all men, it was unreasonable that he, whose profession it was to teach and inculcate these principles, should not be equal to those who are taught ! The Shogun Tsunayoshi acknowledged the justness of this argument, and accordingly ordered that he should no longer be obliged to shave his head, conferred on him the secular title of the fifth rank, and made him president of the college. Upon this, his disciples, who had also shaved their heads, now, following in their master's footsteps, allowed their hair to grow. And all the scholars throughout the empire copied this change of custom. The professors of Confucianism who served the shogun's government at this time had all received their education from Tokushin. The Shogun Tsunayoshi, thus showing his liking for men of letters, incited all the daimios to vie with each other in inviting Confucian scholars to their dominions. Literature had never since ancient times been in so flourishing a condition. In this state of affairs the Shogun Tsunayoshi died, and was succeeded by Iyenobu. Iyenobu took into his favor Arai Kimiyoshi, and consulted him upon the important affairs of the state ; but the opinions of Tokushin were different from those of Kimiyoshi ; the latter, therefore, repeatedly sought permission to retire from office. On this account he received orders to compose works on the organization of offices and ranks, on the particular forms to be observed on occasions of mourning, and works on genealogy. After the death of the Shogun Iyenobu, Kimiyoshi withdrew from office, and Tokushin again occupied himself with the more important business of the state.

He served five shoguns in succession ; in the eighth year of Kioho (A. D. 1723) he resigned the office of president of the college in favor of his son, and was made honorary secretary. He died in the eighty-eighth year of his age. His posterity were successively appointed to the office of president of the college, and they held supreme sway in the literary world. During the shogunate of Iyenari, Matsudaira Norihira was adopted into the Hayashi family, and succeeded to the hereditary office. He aided the shogun's prime-minister, Matsudaira Sadanobu, in the most important affairs of state, and corrected many abuses of the time. Up to his time Hayashi's school had remained a private institution in the possession of the Hayashi family, although its expenses were defrayed by the Government ; but now a national school was established by the Government, and held as government property. To this school Norihira presented his books, and annexed the halls of his old school. At length the Taiseiden, with the school-rooms and halls, was rebuilt, and new school regulations, modes of examination, and systems of gradation, were adopted. According to the old regulations, no one but the retainers of the shogun had been allowed to enter the school; but now another hall was erected, to which the people at large were admitted for study. Moreover, the learned Shibano Hikosuke, Bito Riyosuke, and Koga Yasuke, were engaged and made professors. Ever since the time of the Shogun Iyenobu, learning had been encouraged and cared for, so that now it was in a more flourishing condition than ever. Since the time when the Tokugawa family had founded their government in Yedo, no shoguns had paid so much attention to the cultivation of Chinese philosophy and literature as Tsunayoshi and Iyenobu. The latter, more especially, took pains to root out the warlike spirit which the people had inherited from early times; and with this end in view he established rules of etiquette and dress. The management of these matters he confided to the care of Arai Kimiyoshi, who, comparing ancient precedents with the practice of modern times, drew up regulations on these subjects.

Kimiyoshi, or Hakuseki, by which name he is more generally known, received his education from Kinoshita Junnan.

Junnan was a native of Kioto, and was distinguished for his great learning. He first served the Prince of Kaga, and then the shogun's government, by whom he was employed as a professor. Junnan had many noted disciples; they, together with the Hayashi family, wielded supreme power in the literary world. Among these Kimiyoshi was especially favored by the Shogun Iyenobu, receiving daily additional marks of his esteem and favor.

Kimiyoshi wrote the genealogical records of three hundred and eighty-seven daimios, commencing from the beginning of the period Keicho (A. D. 1596–1614), and ending in that of Yempo (A. D. 1673–1680), during which eighty years all the events which occurred to these daimios are minutely chronicled. He eventually was made governor of the province Chikugo, with the fifth rank. He died in the tenth year of Kioho (A. D. 1723), in the sixty-ninth year of his age, having during his life written on more than three hundred different subjects.

Muro Naokiyo, otherwise known as Kinso, also, like his teacher Junnan, served the Prince of Kaga, but, being recommended to the shogun's government by Kimiyoshi, was employed by it as a professor.

When Yoshimune, Prince of Kii, was chosen successor of Iyenobu, his first act was the encouragement of literature. A lecture-hall was constructed at the Takakura Mansion, and Naokiyo was selected as the first court-lecturer. The duties of the holder of this title were, to deliver lectures to the shogun in his court. Yoshimune directed Naokiyo to translate from Chinese into Japanese the work of Chinese moral philosophy, which he caused to be published and distributed to the writing-masters in the city, to be used as copies for their young pupils. Naokiyo also translated the Chinese ethics, viz., the five human relations of father and son, master and servant, husband and wife, of friends, and of brothers; and the five cardinal virtues, humanity, uprightness, propriety, wisdom, and sincerity. He died in the nineteenth year of Kioho (A. D. 1734), aged seventy-seven years. Among the works which survived him are forty-three volumes of his essays.

It will be seen that, during the period of Kioho (A. D. 1716–1735) the two families of Hayashi and Kinoshita educated more learned scholars than all the other teachers. And, as in accordance with the maxim "What the superior loves the inferior will be found to love more," there was not a province in which learning was not cultivated, nor a family in which books were not read. At Kioto there were Ito Jinsai and his sons, and at Yedo Butsu Sorai, who were all considered ornaments of the period.

Sorai, commonly called Ogin Soyemon, was born in Yedo. He was a retainer of Yanagisawa Yoshiyasu, who was a favorite of the Shogun Tsunayoshi. On every occasion that the shogun visited Yoshiyasu, Soyemon had the honor of delivering in his presence lectures on the Chinese classics. Among Sorai's disciples were many men of excellence. They all upheld the old doctrines of the Chinese classics, and spread their fame abroad.

Jinsai, whose every-day name was Ito, established at Horikawa, in Kioto, a private boarding-school, and devoted himself to the education of students for upward of forty years; every province of the empire, except the three of Hida, Sado, and Iki, contributed pupils to his school, and their total summed up to more than three thousand. The Prince of Higo, hearing of his fame, offered him, on the condition of his entering his service, a yearly income of one thousand kokus of rice; but Ito declined the prince's proposal. In the second year of Ho-ei (A. D. 1705) Ito died, aged seventy-nine. Among his works are to be found the comments on the "Confucian Analects" and "Mencius," the books of "Divination," and several others. He had five sons, and was succeeded by the eldest, Genzo. The second was Juzo, who served the Prince of Fukuyama. Shozo was the third; he served the Prince of Takatsuki. The fourth was Heizo; he served the Prince of Kurume. The youngest was Saizo; he served the Prince of Kii. They were thus employed by the princes on account of the literary knowledge which they had acquired from their father. They were called the five Zos of Ito, from the final syllable of their common names.

Genzo's works were very considerable, the following being among the number, "Teaching of Old Learning," the "Changes in Old Learning," and more than fifty others, which are considered of great utility. There is also besides these a collection of his essays. He died in the first year of Genbun (A. D. 1736), in the sixty-seventh year of his age.

From the above-mentioned facts it will be seen that literature was in a very prosperous condition. On this account school rules and regulations, together with methodical courses of lectures, were regularly established, and these became the foundation of the future educational system.

Soon after many useful institutions, such as the Observatory, the Medical School, and the School for Western Medicine, were gradually established. This state of things naturally arose from the increased civilization of the times, as well as from the attention which the Tokugawa family devoted to the promotion of literature.

We will now enter upon the historical records of the institutions connected with astronomy, medicine, etc., and, in order more completely to show their origin, short biographies of those who were more particularly concerned with them will be added to the description of each institution.

Astronomical Institutions.—The first observatory was that of Kanda, which was erected in the first year of Yenkio (A. D. 1744).

The Shogun Yoshimune had already, while still leading a private life in the residence of the Prince of Kii, shown an inclination for the study of astronomy and calendrical science, and after he had succeeded to the shogunate he sent for Tatebe Hikojiro, in order that he might personally obtain from him information upon such subjects. He also caused a large celestial globe to be made under the direction of Kato, who was a skillful artificer, and was for this purpose called from the province of Kii. In the third year of Kioho (A. D. 1718) Yoshimune himself made an apparatus for determining the sun's meridian altitude, and he placed it in his garden of Fukiage. He also, hearing of Nishigawa Joken, who was well versed both in astronomy and calendrical science, called him from Nagasaki, and requested him to present his works. In the same year, the first year of Yenkio (A. D. 1744), a new observatory was built, in which the celestial globe, which had been constructed, was placed.

In the third year of Yenkio (A. D. 1746) Nishigawa Chiujiro, the son of Joken, having been ordered to correct the Teikio almanac, which Yasui Santetsu had composed from his own calculations, and which had been found to be incorrect, published an amended almanac. Santetsu was originally a skillful player at "go" (an intricate game of checkers, introduced from China); but, possessing natural talents for mathematics, had discovered, upon comparison, that the sun's actual position and motions did not always correspond with the place and motions indicated in the almanac which had been in use since the fourth year of Jokuwan (A. D. 862), during a period of eight hundred and twenty-odd years. He, therefore, had compiled a new and corrected one, which had been distributed throughout the empire under the name of Teikio almanac. On this account he was in that year made astronomer to the Government.

In the second year of Kuwanyen, four years after the retirement from office of the Shogun Yoshinobu, the almanac (calculated, as above mentioned, by Nishigawa Chiujiro) was completed. In this country, however, all matters of a calendrical nature had, in accordance with law, been managed, from age to age, by the Tsuchimikado family. Hence this new and corrected almanac was subjected to the examination of Abe Yasukuni, and his approval of the corrections was requested, upon which Yasukuni went through the ceremony of an astronomical calculation on the winter solstice of the third year of Horeki (A. D. 1753), to participate in which the author came from Yedo.

In the following year this almanac was published and distributed among the people. Soon afterward the astronomical office was abolished, although the three families of Shibukawa, Nishigawa, and Yoshida, still continued to direct astronomical subjects. In the second year of Meiwa (A. D. 1765), Yoshida Shiro founded at Ushigome an office for compiling new almanacs. Eighteen years later, or in the second year of Temmei (A. D. 1782), this office was removed to Asakusa, where a new observatory was built. The revised almanac, distributed in the fourteenth year of Tempo (A. D. 1843), was calculated at this observatory.

Medical Schools.—A medical school was first founded on the Chinese system in the second year of Meiwa (A. D. 1765), by Taki Genko, a physician of the shogun's government.

Genko was a descendant of the family of Yamba; his forefathers were physicians in the service of the imperial court; one of them, however, was a physician of the shogun. Genko distinguished himself greatly in his profession, and in the above-mentioned year he at length asked for and obtained from the Government a piece of ground at Soto Kanda, in Yedo, where he founded a private school, where the younger members of the families of government physicians and the physicians of the several provinces and towns were able to study medical science. In the following year Genko died, and was succeeded by his son Gentoku, who superintended the medical school. In the first year of Anyei (A. D. 1772), this school was burnt down, and Gentoku, at his own expense, rebuilt it. In the second year of Anyei (A. D. 1773), all the physicians in the service of the shogun were ordered to subscribe a certain amount of money toward defraying the expenses of this school. In the sixth year of Temmei (A. D. 1786) the school was again rebuilt, and new regulations were made, by which the children of government physicians·and other students were allowed to live within the school, and carry on their studies during the term of one hundred days in the two seasons of spring and summer of every year. In the third year of Kuwansei (1791) a new system was established, and the school received some land-endowments and became a government medical institution.

The new system was formed under the direction of Anchio, the son of Gentoku. He abolished the practice of admitting the physicians of the provinces and towns, and only admitted members of the families of the government physicians, limiting the age of those admitted to forty years and under. Besides which he fixed days on which all the physicians of the shogun should meet and discuss matters referring to their profession., The office of school-director, however, was still held by Gentoku himself. On this occasion also all the officers of the school, such as supervisors, lecturers, compounders of medicines, etc., were appointed. When any patients sought advice, they were examined by all the physicians of the institution, and were supplied with medicines at the expense of the Government.

Gentoku and Anchio, as a reward for having devoted themselves to this profession, and for having founded, rebuilt, and kept open this school at their own expense, received from the Government a certain sum of money. Since this the posterity of the Taki family have continued to be made directors of this school.

In the third year of Bunkuwa (A. D. 1806) this school was again unfortunately burnt down, when it was removed to another site in Yedo.

A School of Japanese Language and Literature.—A school of Japanese literature was founded first in the fifth year of Kuwansei (A. D. 1793), by Hanawa Homino-ichi. He was born in the county of Kotama, in the province of Musashi, and lost his eyesight while yet a child ; afterward he came to Yedo and was educated under Imajo. He was very fond of the old books of this country, and during several decades searched for those which in the course of time had become scattered and lost. In the fifty-fifth year of his age, he received from the Government a piece of ground at Banchio, in Yedo, where he founded a school of Japanese literature, near which he built a library to keep his books. In the seventh year of Kuwansei (A. D. 1795) his school was endowed with some land, and placed under the direction of the Shohei College.

Homino-ichi classified and arranged 1,273 subjects, about which the old books treated, into one work of 530 volumes, which he published. Afterward he published a continuation of the same, a work of 1,185 volumes, treating upon 2,103 subjects. On this account, in the tenth year of Kuwansei (A. D. 1798), he asked for and obtained a piece of land at South Shinagawa, where he built a warehouse in which the wooden blocks of his publications were kept. In the second year of Bunkuwa (A. D. 1805) it was found that the ground on which his school was built was too small; therefore, the Government granted him the unoccupied piece of ground situated on the eastern side of his school. Here he erected larger school-buildings. In the fourth year of Bunsei (A. D. 1821) Homino-ichi, on account of his advanced age, retired from office, and his son Tadatomi was made school-director in his place. In the following year Homino-ichi died in the seventy-sixth year of his age.

This school which he founded existed till late years, being in the possession of the Hanawa family.

In ancient times in Japan native learning was not cultivated. It was only after the *foreign* learning had spread in this country that *Japanese* learning began to improve.

After letters were introduced, composition came into use, and by means of these letters the various meanings of words were explained; but in these writings the foreign style of composition had to be adhered to. When Chinese learning had made much progress in Japan the native literature was made to imitate it, and even government enactments were in accordance with the Chinese style. Nevertheless, the colloquial language could not be changed, so that, although the Chinese.

style was used for the written language, the spoken language remained as it always had been. Even at the present day the written and spoken languages are different from each other. Before the Japanese middle ages the orthoepic differences between direct and indirect sounds, or pure and impure, were distinctly observed. On this account, that which was written coincided exactly with that which was spoken. As Chinese learning was more universally followed, this ancient precision was gradually lost. Still, during the periods Kanpei (A. D. 889–897) and Yencho (A. D. 923–930) the priest Shoju and Minamoto each published a dictionary, in both of which the definition of the words was very clear, and the spelling in the Japanese alphabet-sounds was particularly good, so that up to this time the deterioration had not been very considerable. After this there were few who studied the correct accents, and none who corrected the faulty pronunciations. Fujiwara Teika, following the profession of poet, established a system of his own for the employment of the Japanese alphabet-sounds, which not only differed from that in ancient use, but also impugned the correctness of ancient books on this subject. This false system, called the "Goshokana," was used for four hundred and fifty years without its errors being discovered by any one. During the period of Yempo (A. D. 1673–1680), the Buddhist priest Keichiu, of Naniwa, fond of Japanese learning, and well acquainted with the old Japanese works, compiled for Prince Mitsukuni, of Mito, the book of twenty-two volumes of comments on ancient poetry. Keichiu's leading argument was: "In the language of my country, the correct or classical and the vulgar, and again the ancient and the modern, are to be distinguished; if these distinctions are not clearly borne in mind, a correct etymology of the Japanese language will be impossible. The most ancient memorial of the language is the 'Collection of Ancient Poetry;' if, therefore, one does not depend upon this work, it will be impossible to explain the source of the language." With this in view he composed the work to correct the errors then current, and he revived the ancient system of orthography with the Japanese alphabet. At this time a Shinto priest of Kioto, Kada Adzuma-maro, also a votary to Japanese learning, lamented that since the middle ages the pronunciation had become incorrect. He composed a work in eighty volumes, for the purpose of correcting this evil. Kamomabuchi, of Totomi, being for his pleasure in Kioto, became a pupil of Adzuma-maro, and acquired a knowledge of Japanese learning. In the second year of Kuwanyen (A. D. 1749) Mabuchi came to Yedo, and entered the service of Councilor Tayasu Munetake. Here he greatly fostered and extended Japanese learning. What he continually impressed upon his students was: "Let us compare the present condition of Japanese learning to agriculture. We find that Keichiu commences and prepares the ground for seed, but does not complete the sowing of the seed; my teacher nearly completes this, but suddenly dies, so that it remains for us to be responsible for the work of harvest; therefore, you must diligently exert yourselves to finish this work." At length Mabuchi, to disseminate his views, put forth several works on Japanese poetry. Afterward he retired from office, and lived at Hamacho. He died in the sixth year of Meiwa (A. D. 1769), at the age of seventy-three.

Moto-ori Nobunaga was a pupil of Mabuchi, and was more especially skilled in Japanese learning. He composed a "History of Old Times" in forty-eight volumes. In this work the Japanese language is about at its best. Moto-ori Nobunaga was from the province Ise. When he read one of the works of Mabuchi he made a written application to him to become one of his pupils; Mabuchi, admiring his earnest desire, encouraged him, and was the cause of his writing his work on history. Besides this he was the author of the work on "words," and many others. He died in the first year of Kiowa (A. D. 1801), at the age of seventy-two, and left two sons, Shiuntei and Taihei, who both followed their father's profession. Shiuntei was the author of works on grammar. About this time, besides Nobunaga, Fuyetani Nari-akira taught this subject at Kioto. Afterward Hirata Atsutane, Ban Nobutomo, and Tachibana Moribe, successively appeared; but these, desiring to improve what was already correct, produced a contrary effect; nevertheless they were sufficiently correct to be called masters.

School of Foreign Languages.—In the second year of Ansei (A. D.

1855), at the base of the ascent of Kudan, in Yedo, a school was built where the Dutch language was to be taught, Koga Zo being appointed director of this school. In the third year of Ansei (A. D. 1856), Sugita Seikei, a subject of the Prince of Obama, and Mitsukuri Gempo, were appointed teachers in this school. In the following year the school was opened and teaching commenced; at first, however, subjects of the shogun only were admitted as students; it was not until some time after that the retainers of the several daimios were admitted. In the first year of Manyen (A. D. 1860) the school was removed to Ogawa-machi, on which occasion English and French, together with the German and Russian languages, were added to the regular course, and a class in chemistry was commenced. Thus the course of instruction in Western learning was gradually made more complete. In the second year of Bunkiu (A. D. 1862) new and larger buildings for the school were erected near Shitotsubashi Gate. Seikei having died in the mean time, Mitsukuri Gempo and Kawamoto Komin, the latter a retainer of the Prince of Kagoshima, having been called to Yedo and made subjects of the shogun, were appointed professors. In the third year of Bunkiu (A. D. 1863) the school was placed under the management of the Shohei College, and named the Kaisei-jo. In this year some students were for the first time sent to study in England, and the study of European mathematics was commenced in the school. In the first year of Kei-o (A. D. 1865) a Dutch professor was engaged to teach natural philosophy and chemistry. At this time students of the English, French, and German languages increased daily, so that it was found necessary to enlarge the school-rooms and to change the rules of instruction.

Early Foreign Scholars.—The first book published on foreign subjects is by Arai Hakuseki, and it was only after the appearance of this work that foreign learning was taken notice of in this country.

The first European nations that had intercourse with Japan were the Portuguese and Dutch. The former for a long time continued their intercourse with the country; but through their intrigue with the local princes of the western coasts they became odious to the Government, and were expelled in the sixteenth year of Kuanyei (A. D. 1639), and forbidden to return.

At this time, as the Dutch were of service to this country in explaining the real intentions and acts of the Portuguese, special permission was granted them to carry on trade, and in the eighteenth year of Kuanyei (A. D. 1641) the port of Nagasaki, in Hizen, was opened, mercantile houses were established, and this was made the seat of commerce with the Dutch. Once a year some one from the Dutch at Nagasaki paid a visit of respect to the shogun's government at Yedo; and on this account a few young men had been educated to act as interpreters. But these had not been allowed to learn the Dutch letters or to read Dutch books, but had been obliged to acquire their knowledge of the Dutch orally.

The Shogun Yoshimune, being deeply interested in his astronomical and calendrical studies, was informed that the Dutch were well versed in these sciences. He, therefore, called Nishigawa Joken, a native of Nagasaki, and questioned him upon these matters.

Upon this the interpreters, Nishi, Yoshio, and others, by mutual agreement, applied to the Government for permission to learn to read and write Dutch. During the period of Kioho (A. D. 1716–1735) this permission was at last granted, and for the first time the Dutch language was learned from books.

The Shogun Yoshimune, having also obtained some Dutch books, so much admired the minuteness of their engravings that he desired to know the meaning of the explanatory text. There was at this time a private individual called Awoki Bunzo, who, being fond of study, had by special permission obtained the use of the government library books. He finally was made Confucian professor to the Government. The government library was also under his care, and he continually urged the benefits to be derived from the use of Dutch works. Upon this the Shogun Yoshimune commanded Bunzo and Noro Genbun to apply themselves to the study of the Dutch language and literature. In view of this these two men were present at the receptions of the annual messenger from Nagasaki, in order to hear the Dutch language spoken, and they found that with the aid of the interpreters they were able to understand the meaning of what was said. But, owing to the peculiarities of the foreign idiom, they found it difficult to comprehend, and were much embarrassed, more especially as it was only once a year that the messenger came. Although they thus studied for several years, they only acquired a knowledge of the alphabet. During the period of Yenpo (A. D. 1673–1680) they received orders to proceed to Nagasaki, where they studied Dutch with Noshi and Yoshio, and eventually acquired an elementary acquaintance with it. Of these four students, Yoshio especially devoted himself to the acquirement of this language, and for the benefit of future students desired to publish a Dutch and Japanese vocabulary; but he died without carrying out his intention. Bunzo remained and continued his studies for several years, acquiring a knowledge of about four hundred words of daily use, of the various shapes of the capitals and small letters, of the foreign way of spelling monosyllables, together with the method of combining syllables into words. He then returned to Yedo. But Yoshimune had died some time before Bunzo's return to Yedo, and his position was not the same as formerly, for he found himself without a teacher, without fellow-learners, and without books to pursue his studies. He could on this account do no more than publish the books, "Dutch Letters," "Dutch Conversation," and others.

At about this time Mayeno Kiotaku, a physician in the service of the Prince of Nakatsu, and a man who aspired after eminence, and was fond of reading strange and curious books, accidentally came across the fragment of a Dutch book. Being desirous to read it, he became a pupil of Bunzo, and Bunzo, admiring his perseverance, taught him all he knew. But the fragment in question was a very difficult one, and, although day and night were devoted to study, but a very small portion of its contents was understood. The Prince of Nakatsu, believing that Kiotaku's desire was good, sent him to Nagasaki, where he learned about six or seven hundred more words and then returned. After this he once more went to Nagasaki, but, owing to the fact that the interpreters only knew a few words, and that none were able to read books or to translate, although for several years he continually sought from them a more perfect knowledge, he failed in acquiring anything but the mere elements of the Dutch language. Finally, Kiotaku secretly acquired a translated vocabulary and several medical works, with which he returned to Yedo. Here, with the aid of what he had learned, as well as by the aid of the new books, he learned a good deal that he had not known before, and after six or seven years, by his own efforts, acquired an adequate knowledge of the Dutch language. He now commenced several translations, and published a number of works compiled from the Dutch. In the third year of Kiyowa (A. D. 1803) he died, at the age of eighty-one years. He was called Rankiwa Sensei.

Before this the family of Katsuragawa had successively, from father to son, been the shogun's court-surgeons. The ancestor of this family was Morishima, a doctor of the Prince of Hirato. He studied under Arashiyama Ho-an, and later changed his surname to Katsuragawa. When the Shogun Iyenobu, before he became shogun, was in Kofu, he sent for Hochiku to be his body-physician. Hochiku afterward became the government doctor. His great-grandson Hosun became a pupil of Awoki Bunzo, and Hoshiu the son of Hosun was very desirous to learn Dutch. He, together with Sujita Genpaku, became a pupil of Riotaku, and they studied diligently. They formed a society called Komei Shuja, and assisted each other, hoping thus to acquire a perfect knowledge of the Dutch. Gempaku was the physician of the Prince of Obama, and his father, Hosun, had at first learned Dutch surgery from Nishi Soshun. Gempo, the father of Soshun, was a Dutch interpreter at Nagasaki, and was afterward employed by the shogun's government as a physician. Gempaku having obtained a Dutch anatomical work, was desirous of practically comparing its teachings with the ancient Japanese beliefs on this subject. It opportunely happened at this time that the Government had ordered the *post-mortem* examination of an executed criminal to be held, and Gempaku, together with Kiyotaku, undertaking the work, found that the drawings in the Dutch book exactly corresponded with the real organs. From this it was found that the old beliefs were incorrect. He desired, therefore, to have this anatomical work translated and brought to the aid of medical science. But Gempaku did not even have an elementary knowledge of Dutch; on this account, Kiotaku was made chief, and thus the work was in a fair way of being commenced. The help of the interpreters was not desired. But, as a member of the committee of translation, Gempaku was at a loss where to commence. He first applied himself to learning the Dutch alphabet, and thus went on till he gradually acquired a knowledge of words. At last the actual work of translation was commenced; but sometimes the translation of a single word would occupy more than a day, and sometimes several days were needed to translate one sentence. In view of these difficulties, the members of the committee declared that the work could not possibly be achieved; but Gempaku said, "It is possible for man to do it, but it must be with the help of Heaven." The days for carrying on this work were fixed, and Hoshiu, Nakagawa Junan, Mine Shiunotai, Toriyama Shoyen, and Kiriyama Shotetsu, formed themselves into a regular society. Without once ceasing, these men consulted and worked together year after year; the quantity translated increased, and they gradually, and unaided by others, acquired a knowledge of the peculiarities of the Dutch language, so that in each successive year some discrepancies were discovered in the translations done in the preceding year. In this way, during a period of four years, the rough sheets were rewritten not less than eleven different times before the work was finished at last. This work was called "A New Work on Analytical Anatomy." It was engraved and published, and a copy presented to the shogun's government, and to the principal nobles in Kioto. From this the people of the empire learned that it was possible to translate Dutch books, and they learned, besides, the truth respecting the human frame; all this they owed to the energy and perseverance of Gempaku.

At about this time Otsuki Moshitsu, a native of Sendai, hearing that Gempaku was engaged in translating a work on anatomy, came to Yedo, and became a pupil of Gempaku, and a member of the translating society. If he had not believed in the practicability of his work, he would not have joined in it, and he was a man who only wrote what he thoroughly understood. Gempaku, admiring these sterling qualities, helped and encouraged him, and thus contributed to the development of his talents. Moshitsu had in view, not only the medical science, but also the examination of the Dutch grammar, and Dutch books in general. He left Gempaku, and became a pupil of Kiotaku, who, also admiring the earnestness of Moshitsu, taught him without any reserve all he knew. Nevertheless, all this did not satisfy Moshitsu. He therefore left Kiotaku, and proceeded to Nagasaki, where he more fully studied and examined various Dutch works. He then returned to Yedo, and published the work "Steps to the Dutch Language." Before this, Awoki, Mayeno and others had also composed books on the Dutch language, but none had been published. Each of these persons had his own peculiar method of translating according to his own ideas of the grammar of the Dutch language. Their knowledge had been acquired entirely by rote, and not from systematic books. They were, therefore, unable to express correctly the sounds; nor were they more successful in syllabification. But the work treated comprehensively of the combination of vowels with consonants, and of several syllables into words, the main principles involved in the structure of the language and the correct method of translating. It became, therefore, now possible for all Japanese to learn to read and understand Dutch books. In consequence of this a large number of people eminent for talent and ability, seeing this book, became desirous to study the Dutch language. The following people came to Yedo and became pupils of Moshitsu: Udagawa Genzui, a doctor of Tsuyama; Inamoura Sampaku, a doctor of Tottori; Yamamoura Saisuke, a Samarai of Tsuchi-ura; Yasuoka Genshin, a native of Ise; Hashimoto Tokichi, of Osaka, and others. In the fourth year of Bunkwa (A. D. 1807) difficulties with the Russians took place in the northern parts of the empire. In the following year the appearance of the English-on the western coast caused considerable commotion. The Shogun's government decided, therefore, to make itself acquainted with the condition of these two countries, and Moshitsu received orders to compile an account of these countries from the Dutch books. Accordingly, he composed the works in regard to the Russian questions. In the eighth year the shogun's government paid Moshitsu twenty ingots of silver, and continued this payment yearly, making him translator of Dutch works. In the fifth year of Bunsei (A. D. 1822) he at length received a monthly salary. The above was the first instance of the shogun's government directly encouraging Western learning.

The works of Moshitsu were very numerous, and with, a spirit similar to that of Gempaku, he published the revised edition of the new work on "Analytical Anatomy," which entered minutely into the details of the science. He also published "Strange News of the Seas" and "Miscellaneous Essays," etc. In the tenth year of Bunsei (A. D. 1827), he died, aged seventy-one years. His son Genkan followed with success his father's profession. He, too, received commands from the shogun's government to translate Dutch works. He published a small work, which explained the peculiarities of Dutch composition; this was the first work purely on grammar. Besides this he published, also, works on the proper pronunciation of Dutch. At this time there were not a few others besides Genkan who made Dutch learning their occupation. Among these was Awoki Rinso, who, devoting himself to natural philosophy, published a work on the subject. This was the first work on natural philosophy. Kawamoto Komin was a pupil of Rinso, and published an enlarged edition of the work on natural philosophy. Yasuoka Genshin followed this by publishing a work which described the functions of the external and internal organs of the human body. To Genshin is due the merit of advancing medical science. His son Yo-an published the first book on chemistry. Mitsukuri Gempo, of the same clan as Genshin, placed himself under him as his pupil. Gempo devoted himself to geography and history, and published the works on those subjects. His son Seigo also composed a work on geography. The son of Gempaku, Hakugen, acquired his father's learning and communicated it to his son Seikei. This Seiki was eminent for his great talents and extensive knowledge, having finished his studies while still young. He composed works on military subjects. All the above-mentioned men devoted their energies entirely to foreign learning.

Foreign Medical Science.—There was in Yedo an institution called the Western Medical Science School. During the period called Tempo (A. D. 1830–1843), Ito Gemboku, a doctor in the service of the Prince of Saga, Totsuka Teikwai, in the service of the Prince of Kagoshima, Otsuki Shunsai, in the service of the Prince of Sendai, Hayashi Tokai, in the service of the Prince of Kokura, Takenouchi Gendo, in the service of the Prince of Maru-oka, established themselves severally in Yedo, and practised medicine successfully on European principles. A little later, in the hope of arresting the great mortality among Japanese children of both sexes, they added vaccination to their other practice. In the fifth year of Ansei (A. D. 1858), the above-mentioned doctors having formed themselves into a society, established, with the permission of the Government, a private institution for vaccination. During this year the Shogun Iyesada being sick, sent for Gemboku, Gendo, and Teikwai, and made them his court-physicians. This is the first instance in which physicians of the European school, who were not also surgeons, were appointed to the dignity of court-physicians. Upon being appointed to this rank, they made over to the Government their vaccination institution. Shunsai and Tokai being made directors of the institution, three classes of students were established, i. e., a general medical class, an anatomy class, and a vaccination class, and Ishikawa Osho, Tsuboi Shindo, and others, were appointed teachers. The following year, this institution having been burnt, a new one was built, to which was attached a lecture-room, and chambers for use of the pupils, and Shunsai was made sole director. The current expenses of this institution were borne by the Government. In the first year of Bunkiu (A. D. 1861) the institution, in order to distinguish it from another medical school where Chinese medical art was taught, was named the European Medical School. In the second year of Bunkiu (A. D. 1862) a chemical department was added to the institution, and a class for physiology was formed, and physiological works were published. In this year the director, Shunsai, died, and his son Genohun was appointed in his place, Gemboku, Gendo, and Tokai, being appointed to advise him. Later on Ogata Ko-an was sent from Osaka to replace these three. Previous to this, Matsumoto Riojun and others had been sent to Nagasaki to study medicine with a Dutch physician. Afterward Gempaku, the son of Gemboku, and Kenkai, the son of Tokai, were sent to Holland to study medicine. Later on Riojun opened a medical school at Nagasaki, which was entirely built and conducted in accordance with the Dutch system.

In the first year of Genji (A. D. 1864) Ko-an died, and to replace him Riojun was called from Nagasaki, and he reformed and amended the rules and regulations of the institution, and made it much more prosperous.

The medical school at Nagasaki was opened in the first year of Bunkiu (A. D. 1861), Matsumoto Riojun having obtained the permission of the shogun's government for this purpose. At this time it was only at Nagasaki that medical students received foreign instruction, and the teachers in all cases were Dutch doctors. Riojun having learned from the Dutch doctors the rules and regulations of military and public hospitals, established for the first time at Nagasaki a hospital. Although the principal object was the healing of the sick, still a medical class was attached to it, and a medical professor was engaged from Holland which increased its prosperity greatly. After this Riojun was called to Yedo, to take office in the medical school. In the first year of Kei-o (A. D. 1865), Natural Philosophy and Chemistry class-rooms were added to the Nagasaki Medical School, and a Dutch professor was engaged to teach these sciences.

In the third year of Bunkiu (A. D. 1863) there was also established at Nagasaki a foreign-language school, at which the five following languages were taught by professors engaged from each of the countries named, i. e., Chinese, Dutch, English, French, and Russian. The division into classes and the manner of teaching were such as prevailed in the several countries from which the professors had been obtained. Later on mathematics were also taught. At this time one of the professors, an American, having an extensive knowledge of Japanese, was a very successful instructor, so that the number of students increased greatly.

The above-mentioned institutions and schools, together with the Osaka Medical School and the Hakodate Hospital, were all established by the shogun's government. At the time of the restoration, the Imperial Government took over these institutions, revised and improved the regulations, and enlarged their scope. At the present day these are the centres from which scientific knowledge is diffused.

Printing under the Shoguns.—During the sixteenth century the political troubles in the empire and contests of warlike factions resulted in the destruction of most of the educational institutions of the empire. Books which had been gathered into libraries, or collected in private houses, were scattered or destroyed. A military spirit sprung up in the country, which was unfavorable to the cultivation of literature and the production of books.

Previous to this period, the art of printing had made considerable progress in the country. As early as the fourth year of Jingo Kei-un (A. D. 770) the Empress Koken had caused to be prepared a large edition of the Buddhist canonical book, and distributed it among the Buddhist temples throughout the empire. This book was printed from the wooden blocks in the ordinary style of printing Chinese and Japanese. In this method of printing, a block is made for each page of the book, which is used like a stereotype plate of the present day. These blocks are made from wood, by cutting away the intervals between the letters and leaving the face of the letters standing in relief. For the purpose of printing from these blocks they are laid face upward on a flat table. The ink is put on with the flat brush. Then the sheet of paper is laid upon the face of the block, and pressed down upon it by means of a soft pad or rubber. A single block contains two pages. The paper is printed only on one side, and then folded into a single leaf.

Printing with movable types was probably introduced into Japan in the sixteenth century, but was never extensively used until a very recent time. These types at first were made from wood, but now are made from type-metal in the usual manner.

Printing with movable type is a matter of more difficulty in the Japanese language than in European languages. Ordinary books require at least five thousand different types. In spite of these difficulties, however, movable types have been extensively introduced, and all of the newspapers are now printed with them.

Accession to power of the Tokugawa family restored peace to the country, and was followed by a great revival in the printing and collection of books. The great historical works which were undertaken under the patronage of the shogun and different daimios were printed with blocks at their expense.

A class of booksellers and book-publishers grew up in the country, and a regular system of copyright and censorship is found to have existed for the last two centuries.

Provincial and Private Schools under the Shoguns.—Toward the close of the Ashikaga dynasty, ambitious and warlike leaders sprung up in every part of Japan, and divided the country among themselves; the more powerful continually sought to increase their dominions, consequently an unceasing state of warfare prevailed; the larger absorbed the smaller, and the more powerful subdued the weaker. For a long time this unsettled condition prevailed, until Ota Nobunaga and Toyotomi Hideyoshi, by their superior prowess, brought them all to a state of subjection. From this time dates the commencement of the feudal system. Although the daimios were subdued, still they each in their several countries ruled their retainers by their own laws, and in each country the education of the young was encouraged by the chiefs. In the following pages is a brief account of the most prominent means employed for this purpose.

In the fifteenth year Tenshio (A. D. 1587), Toyotomi Hideyoshi reduced the country of Satsuma to a state of obedience; and at this time he made Kobaya Kawa feudal lord of the province of Chikuzen. This prince fostered and encouraged education in his province, and established a school, on the plan of the Ashikaga College, in Shimotsuke. Owing to the unsettled state of the country, learning had been universally neglectĕd, and nobody paid attention to it except Kobaya Kawa, and he was the first who took measures for the education of the military class. Nevertheless, after his death this school seems to have been neglected, so that it is difficult now to find out the rules and regulations that once were in force there.

In Yechigo, the feudal lord, Uyesugi Kagekatsu, and his son of the same name, were fond of learning; and Naoye Kanetsugu, their retainer, too, was desirous that the education of the people should be encouraged. Afterward Kagekatsu was transferred to Dewa. Here he established a school where his retainers received instruction. Afterward Harunori, the grandson of Kagekatsu, reformed and enlarged this school so much, that it became celebrated throughout the north and east.

Toshitsune, the son of Mayeda Toshinaga, who had received the three provinces of Kaga, Noto, and Yechiu, as his dominion, established schools where the young men of his retainers were taught literature and military science. At a later period Toshitsune retired to the castle of Komatsu, where he established a local school.

Ikeda Terumasa, the feudal lord of Bizen, was a great admirer of literature, and intrusted the government of his country to the scholar Kumazawa Riokai. In the ninth year of Kuambun (A. D. 1669) he established a new school called Shirutane, open to the civil and military classes. To this school was attached a department for teaching military exercises. Besides the above-mentioned schools, the other fiefs were not without their schools. In these schools, although the rules were various, still the principles of education were equally recognized in all. The principal and most prosperous among these schools were in Owari, Mito, Saga, Kumamoto, Kagoshima, Sendai, Aidzu, Hagi, Kubota, and Ise. In each of these rules were established, classes formed, and the young of the province taught. On this account it is not surprising that at the present day learned scholars and men of talent abound in these provinces.

The above is an account of the schools established by the feudal lords after the ascendency of the Tokugawa dynasty; but as yet there were few private schools that had attained to any celebrity, although learned men had devoted themselves to teaching scholars collected around them, and had opened boarding-schools, where literature and penmanship were taught. Although private schools did not flourish, we must bear in mind that they lacked the encouragement and support of the local government. Among them there were some that were continued from generation to generation in the same family. Those that became most flourishing and were regarded with the greatest respect in Japan, were one in Kioto founded by Ito Itei, and one in Osaka founded by Nakai Shin-an. Itei in his youth embraced the classical teachings of the Chinese authors of the period of So, and he was the author of two works on philosophy; but later he came to believe that the Chinese authors, Tei and Shu, did not express in their writings the true and original meaning of the Chinese classics. He therefore discontinued their use, and introduced in their place a set of doctrines of his own composition. This school being built in Horikawa, was commonly called and known as the Horikawa School. Choin, the son of Itei, supported the family fame for learning. On the death of Choin, his son Zensho being very young, Choken, the uncle of Zensho, returned from Kii, and for ten years took the direction of the school upon himself, after which Zensho undertook its management. Kii followed his father's example, and by him, too, the reputation of the family name was upheld. This school was carried on by the descendants of the family without a break till the thirteenth year of Tempo (A. D. 1642). By a special order of the Government the land-tax on the school-premises was remitted. From the foundation of the school by Itei to the thirteenth year of Tempo was a period of about ninety years.

In the eleventh year of Kioho (A. D. 1726), Shinan having applied for and obtained the government permission, founded the Osaka City School. At this time Miake Seimei was made master, and Juntei made assistant teacher.

The inhabitants of Osaka being principally devoted to commercial pursuits, learning was not thought of much account by them. The school established by Shuan was the first one opened in that city; and seeing that he selected such competent men as teachers, he deserves great praise. Later Juntei left Osaka and went to Yedo, upon which Shuan himself taught in the school. After a lapse of several years

Juntei returned and resumed his duties in the school. On the death of Shuan and Juntei, Sekizen, the son of Shuan, succeeded his father in the school. Sekizen was noted for his great knowledge and literary powers. He composed an historical work of thirteen volumes, and presented it to the shogun's government. The Government sent in return to Sekizen money for repairs, etc., for his school.

CHAPTER IV.

EDUCATION SINCE THE REVOLUTION.

IN October of the third year of Kei-o (A. D. 1867), the Shogun Tokugawa Keiki resigned into the imperial hands the office which his family had held for more than two hundred and fifty years. During that period the chief executive power had been held by the shogun at his capital in Yedo. The nominal authority had, however, always remained in the person of the mikado, who maintained his court at the imperial capital, Kioto. The change which resulted from the resumption of authority by the mikado affected all departments of the Government. It has required several years of experiment to adapt the forms of government and administration to the altered circumstances. For a time the old adherents of the shogunate resisted by force of arms the cession of power into the imperial hands. But in 1869 all opposition ceased, and since that time the process of reformation in the Government has gone on rapidly and successfully.

A Year-Period adopted.—In the year 1868, on the death of the old mikado, and the accession of his son, the present mikado, the year-name was changed to Meiji. This system of a year-name was borrowed from China, and the changes were made at frequent and irregular intervals. Some lucky or unlucky event generally formed the pretext for making the change. In the present instance the period is made to correspond with the reign of the mikado. The first year of Meiji corresponded with the 2528th year of the imperial dynasty, from the accession of Jimmu Tenno, and with the 1868th year of the Christian era.

In the year 1869 the Government was removed from the former capital, Kioto, to Yedo, and, in order that the event might be duly signalized, the new capital was called Tokio.

The new Government early gave its attention to the subject of education, and, in the years of transition which preceded the establishment of the present Department of Education, made many important movements toward giving to the nation an adequate educational system. Some of the most important of the measures we shall proceed to enumerate, premising, however, that, as they were tentative in their character, they were often superseded or modified.

First Educational Measures.—In the third month of 1868, the Imperial Government took its first step in educational matters, by establishing a school in Kioto for the promotion of literature. An organization something like the old national university which had existed in the middle ages was reëstablished, and to it was intrusted the supervision of educational affairs. The theory of this university, it will be remembered, was, that it should serve as a means for training up the young men of the noble classes for public service. It was, moreover, not merely a college for study, but an educational board for the examination and licensure of the candidates for official positions.

In order to train suitable men for the new duties which were now to be devolved upon the Imperial Government, an order was issued urging upon the court nobles the importance of cultivating their talents and acquiring a knowledge which would be of practical use in the official duties which they might be called upon to fulfill; and calling attention to the new educational board which had been organized. The Government also took measures to carry on the educational work which had been begun by the shogun. In the fifth month the foreign-language school at Nagasaki was taken under government protection, and its rules and regulations were reformed. The hospital at Nagasaki was also taken over, and provision made for instruction in medicine. A hospital was also built at Kioto. In the sixth month all the educational institutions in Tokio were taken under government control, teachers were obtained for the medical school, and instruction was commenced. Before this a hospital had been opened at Yokohama, for the treatment of wounded soldiers, which was now removed to Tokio and placed in charge of the medical school. A school of chemistry and physics was established in the city of Osaka, and extensive provision was made for instruction. A temporary military school was also opened at Kioto in the eighth month, especially designed for training the court nobility in the military duties which were now required of them. A Chinese medical school, which had been maintained in Tokio, was now converted into a dispensary for vaccination ; and this, together with an infirmary and other medical institutions, was placed under the direction of the medical school. The College of Confucius, which had attained great fame under the shogunate, was now, after having been suspended on account of the civil war, reopened ; and in the ninth month the Foreign-Language School, which had also been for a time suspended, was resumed, and a room for the discussion of general subjects was opened in connection with it.

Reëstablishment of the University at Kioto.—In this same month an imperial edict was issued directing the establishment of a national university for the promotion of literary and military education. This design, however, was not carried out. The pressure of business made it impossible for the Government to enter upon this scheme at that time. As a temporary expedient, a school for Japanese learning was opened at Kioto, where the court nobles, the government officers, and others, might acquire literary and practical culture. The following are some of the excellent principles promulgated in connection with the establishment of this school :

1. It is incumbent on every citizen to understand the nature of the public institutions of his country, and to become familiar with the duties pertaining to his position in society.

2. Foreign learning, both Chinese and European, must be made to subserve the interests of Japan. The past calamities of the empire have been due to the usurpation of power and the neglect of their appropriate duties on the part of the military chiefs. Hereafter let all adhere strictly and honestly to the duties belonging to their respective stations.

3. Useless styles of composition, and aimless discourses and dis-

cussions, ought to be abandoned in the future methods of education; and the literary and military branches of learning ought to be so cultivated as to be mutually helpful.

4. Japanese and Chinese learning are not antagonistic, and therefore the students of these systems, forgetting their former conflicts, should show forbearance toward each other.

In the latter part of the year 1868 a proclamation was issued to the following effect: "Japanese learning has of late greatly declined, so that the honor of the country in its relations with foreign nations has been materially prejudiced. It is now the intention of the Government to take measures to revive Japanese learning, and it is earnestly desired that every one, by diligent study and by encouraging sound scholarship, should aid in this work."

On the reopening of the Foreign-Language School at Tokio, the buildings formerly used were then occupied as military barracks. Hence temporarily the school occupied other quarters; but, in the twelfth month, it was again put in possession of its own buildings near Shitotsubashi gate.

In the first month of the second year of Meiji (A. D. 1869) the restrictions in regard to rank were abolished in reference to students admitted to the College of Confucius, and to the Foreign-Language School. English and French teachers were engaged for the Foreign-Language School, and the students were separated into two divisions, the first to be taught by foreign teachers, and the second by Japanese.

Publication of Newspapers, etc.—In the third month the publication of newspapers was sanctioned by the Government. This is believed to have been the first public recognition of the modern newspaper, an institution which has received a remarkable development since that time in Japan. The bureau for their management was for a time connected with the Department of Education, but subsequently was transferred to the Department of Home Affairs. At the time of this first sanctioning of newspapers, there was also established a bureau for the compilation and correction of historical records.

In the fourth month a Chinese classical lecture-room was opened at the College of Confucius, in Tokio, at which the court nobles, the daimios, the lesser nobles, and public officers, attended. This was designed as a method of mutual improvement, in order to give to the leading men of the day an opportunity to increase their culture and their knowledge of affairs. There seems to have been a division into classes for the better attainment of their purposes. There was the class of *explanation*, the class of *mutual improvement*, the class of *inquiry*, and the class of *debate*. The attendants were allowed liberty of choice in regard to which of these classes they would join.

Further arrangements were about this time also made for the College of Confucius, and the Foreign-Language School. In each provision was made for three hundred pupils to be boarded and taught. Instruction in the German language was commenced in the Foreign-Language School. New buildings for the School of Chemistry and Physics in Osaka were completed. In the Medical School at Nagasaki, mathematics, physics, and chemistry, were added to the regular course, and a Dutch teacher was engaged to teach these branches.

Educational Regulations.—In the seventh month a government edict was issued, defining the duties of the several officers of the Educational Board. The chief officer of this board was charged with the direction of the higher institutions of learning and of the Board of Historical Compilation, as well as with the general superintendence of the city and provincial schools. The relative ranks in which teachers had before been classed were abolished, and the new ranks of senior, middle, and junior professor, and senior, middle, and junior teacher, were substituted. The officers of all the schools under the direction of the Educational Board were also classified. For each school there were appointed a supervisor of students, a school-monitor, and a clerk. Rules and regulations for the schools were gradually introduced, and a better system of education was thus step by step established.

In the ninth month a hospital and a foreign-language school were established at Osaka. Shortly afterward a regulation was adopted by the Government confirming in their profession all physicians in their service above thirty years of age, and confiding all below that age to the care of the Educational Board for further instruction and examination. A medical school was also opened at Osaka in connection with the hospital at that place. The medical establishments in Tokio where the Chinese and Japanese systems were taught were placed in the charge of the Educational Board, and provision was made for instruction to be given by competent native physicians.

In the first month of the third year of Meiji (A. D. 1870) additional regulations were issued in regard to the admission of students to the Foreign-Language School at Tokio, and to the National University. As the latter of these give some idea of the views of education which prevailed at that time, we add a summary of them as follows :

1. *Principles of Learning.*—The principles of law exist in all things, and have so existed from all time. They show themselves in the three natural relations which bind society together, viz., justice between master and servant, affection between father and son, and the affection between husband and wife. They also are manifest in the five cardinal virtues of humanity, viz., humanity, uprightness, propriety, wisdom, and sincerity. In public affairs they serve to secure good administration in civil and criminal cases. A school is an institution in which these principles are taught, so that they may be practically followed throughout the country. It is essential that in the young men of a nation should be inculcated the principles of filial piety, of brotherly love, of the just relations between master and servant, parent and child, husband and wife, and brethren and friends. It is equally essential that they should be educated in all the domestic and public virtues, so that the duties which relate to the state and to individuals may both be faithfully performed.

2. *Educational System.*—Near the imperial residence a university has been established. In each of the cities and provinces middle and elementary schools will be organized under regulations issued by the university. In these, talents which may eventually be of service to the state will be cultivated. The university is designed to be the culminating point at which the most advanced students may be collected, and

where their education may be completed. For admission to the university the full quota of studies in the lower schools must be finished, and an examination passed.

3. *Regulations for sending Students from the Provinces to the University.*—The limit as to age will be thirty years. The local examination must be passed and a government certificate obtained. Those admitted are to have the title of "university students." Liberty of selecting the course of study is to be allowed, but when selected the course to be pursued throughout. The duration of a course in the university is to be three years, after which the students return to their own provinces. In case of vacancy students are to be admitted from the local schools.

4. *Manner of Examination.*—Examinations are to be held in the middle months of spring and autumn. The students are to be examined upon those branches which they have pursued. They are also to be required to prepare an original essay upon some assigned subject. The results of these examinations are to be compared by the teachers. If any exhibit unusual talent, and their conduct has also been without fault, they are to be reported specially to the Government, in order that if their services are required they may be appointed to office.

5. *School Expenses.*—The amount to be allowed for educational purposes in each city and province is to be fixed in proportion to their local revenues.

6. *Departments of Study.*—In the university there shall be five departments of study, each having its respective branches as follows:

(1.) *Religion.*—Shinto doctrines; moral philosophy.

(2.) *Law.*—Politics; civil law; commercial law; criminal law; civil procedure; international law; political economy; regulations of court etiquette; statistics.

(3.) *Science.*—Physics; astronomy; geology; mineralogy; zoölogy; botany; chemistry; mechanical power; machinery; mathematics; surveying; architecture.

(4.) *Medicine.*—In the preparatory division, mathematics; physics; chemistry; mineralogy; zoölogy; botany; metrology. In the principal division, anatomy; physiology; artiology; acology; toxicology; post-mortem examinations; medical jurisprudence; surgery; therapeutics; hygiene.

(5.) *Literature.*—History; biography; literature; philosophy.

Rules were also made for the middle and elementary schools. For the elementary schools the pupils were to be between eight and fifteen years of age; and for the middle schools, from sixteen years upward. The studies assigned were reading, penmanship, arithmetic, geography, and foreign languages. In the last part of the middle-school course they were to be taught the elements of one of the courses of study assigned for the university. Selections were to be made for the entrance to the university in accordance with the talents displayed. A selection of books to be read in each of the departments was made, and the students required to read and study these.

Astronomy and the compilation of the national almanac had for many generations been the special pursuit of the family of Tsuchi-Mikado. The old observatory which had existed at Yedo had already been abolished. In order to provide for this branch of science, an office was established in connection with the university, where the calculations for the almanacs were made, and from which they were annually distributed.

Revision of the Educational System.—In the summer of this year, so much discussion arose in regard to educational matters, that it was thought necessary to remodel the entire system, and for this purpose an imperial edict was issued, temporarily closing the schools, and sending the students to their homes. The Foreign-Language School at Tokio was continued, and the local authorities of the provinces were required to send their quotas of students. The number to be sent from each province was determined according to its population. Several students were at the same time sent abroad for the purpose of pursuing their education.

In the twelfth month all venders of medicines were required to have their stock examined by the medical school, and to apply for a license to sell them. All persons desiring to open private schools, or to engage in teaching the arts and sciences, were also required to procure permission from the local governments.

Originally the students in foreign countries had been under the care of the Department of Foreign Affairs. They were sent in some cases by departments of the Government, and in other cases by the local governments of the provinces to which they belonged. Others, again, went abroad as students at their private expense. In consequence of these several methods of sending students, they were of various degrees of talent, age, and advancement. For these reasons the care and direction of these students for the future were intrusted to the Educational Board. New regulations were made for their management. Each was required to obtain a permit before going abroad. A distinction was made between those who were sent by the Government and those who went at their own option. All, however, were put under the care of the Japanese diplomatic agents in the countries where they resided. Several students this year were sent from the Foreign-Language School at Tokio. The imperial prince, Higashi Fushimi, and other members of the imperial family, were sent out as students, as well as some of the sons of the higher nobility.

In the first month of the fourth year of Meiji (A. D. 1870), a classroom was opened in the Tokio Foreign-Language School for the study of the German language. A Prussian was employed as a teacher, and thirty students were admitted to study German. In the second month a school was opened in connection with the Department of Foreign Affairs, for learning the Chinese and European languages. This was designed to train young men in these languages who might serve the department in the necessary intercourse with the foreign countries with which they were connected by treaty.

Establishment of a Department of Education.—In the seventh month of this year (A. D. 1870), the most important step was taken in the modification of the educational machinery of Japan. The old organization, modeled after the idea of the university of the middle ages, and which we have denominated the Educational Board, was abolished. Its university functions had never in reality been exercised, and it had only served the purpose of a bureau of administration.

In connection with the changes which at this time were made in all the departments of government, educational affairs were also assigned to a distinct department, called the Mombusho, or Department of Education. It had charge of the general management of all educational matters, whether connected with the upper, middle, or lower schools. It had power to make and change rules and regulations for schools; to open, close, divide, and unite them; to organize school districts; to take charge of the erection of school-buildings; to engage teachers, and to regulate the expenses of schools. This department had also charge of all affairs connected with medicine and medical education, and of the matter of licensing and regulating the publication of books and periodicals. All the institutions of learning which had been established in the capital and in other cities were transferred to this new department.

The officers of this department entered upon their work with energy and discretion. At first only unimportant and casual changes were made. Meanwhile a more comprehensive scheme of national education was matured and at a later date was initiated.

In this same month anatomical lectures were begun by a German professor at the Tokio Medical School. Other foreign professors were subsequently added, and the instruction of a large body of students in medicine according to the Western system was fairly inaugurated.

The want of proper text-books to enable the Department of Education to carry out its plans was severely felt. The old text-books used under the pure Japanese system were not sufficient to teach the arts and sciences of modern times. A Bureau of Book Compilation was therefore organized in the department, to which were joined the lexigraphic-office and the translating-office which had existed under the old Educational Board. The offices of translation which had been established in the Foreign-Language School and the Medical School of Tokio were also consolidated with this bureau. Men versed in foreign languages and sciences were here employed to compile and prepare works suitable to be used for text-books in the schools of the empire.

An Embassy to Foreign Countries.—The fourth year of Meiji (A. D. 1871) was not marked by any important changes in educational matters. It was during this year that the embassy headed by Iwakura, junior prime-minister, was dispatched to America and Europe. One of the objects aimed at in this embassy was an investigation of the educational institutions and administration of these countries. One of the embassadors was specially charged with the duty of studying and reporting upon education. Tanaka Fujimaro also accompanied the embassy as a special commissioner on this subject. He was absent during the whole of the year 1872, and visited the leading nations, and made an examination into their educational systems. The results were embodied in an extended report, and in the code of education which was subsequently prepared. In January, 1872, measures were taken to collect a museum of articles to be sent to the Vienna International Exhibition. The collection proved so extensive and interesting to the public that, after making a selection to be sent to Vienna, the remainder were kept open as a public museum. This was the beginning of the present extensive Tokio Museum. It afterward received large accessions, both by further collections of native articles and by foreign articles obtained by purchase or exchange at Vienna.

In the same month press-laws were issued by the Department of Education for the regulation of the printing and publication of books and periodicals. It was thereby enacted that, for the publication of any book, a government license must be obtained; that the publication of all matter which impugned established laws, or was libelous or contrary to sound morals, was prohibited; that the pirating of published works of other authors was forbidden.

In the second month the first female school was opened in Tokio. The course of study included the English language. Besides this, a schedule of subjects was provided similar to that in the elementary schools. The teachers were in part foreign and in part Japanese ladies.

In the fifth month steps were taken to organize a normal school for training teachers for the elementary schools of the empire. The want of competent teachers who could carry on the schools in accordance with the present requirements of education was greatly felt. The old teachers had been accustomed to the Chinese methods, and were unskilled in foreign science and knowledge. This normal school was the first step in the work of providing a better-trained class of teachers. A sufficient number of suitable candidates presented themselves for admission, and the school was accordingly opened. An American teacher, familiar with the organization and methods employed in such institutions, was engaged to introduce a proper system of instruction.

Code of Education.—The deliberations of the Department of Education resulted, in the seventh month A. D. 1872, in the issue of an important code of education. It was intended to include the principles and regulations necessary for all classes of schools in the empire. In the subsequent years it has been found necessary to alter and amend this code in many particulars, but in the main it has proved a valuable and satisfactory manual for the administration of school affairs. The following extract is given from the introduction to this important document:

" The acquirement of knowledge and the cultivation of talent are essential to a successful life. By education men learn to acquire property, practise learned professions, perform public services, and make themselves independent of the help of their fellow-men. Schools are designed to provide this essential education. In their various capacities they are intended to supply to all classes of men the knowledge necessary for a successful life. The simple forms of language, the methods of writing, the principles of calculation, the highest knowledge of law, politics, science and arts, the preparation of the officer for his duties, of the farmer and merchant for their occupations, the physician for his profession, all of these it is the proper function of schools to supply. Poverty and failure in the careers of life find their chief cause in the want of education.

" Although schools have been established for many centuries in Japan, yet so far as they have been provided by government they have been confined to the military retainers and to the upper classes. For the lower classes of society, and for women, learning was regarded as beyond their sphere, and, if acquired at all, was of a limited character. Even among the higher classes the character of education was defective. Under the pretext of acquiring knowledge for the benefit of the state, much time was spent in the useless occupation of writing poetry and composing elegant maxims, instead of learning what would be for their own benefit or that of the state.

"Recently an improved educational system has been formed, and the methods of teaching remodeled. It is designed henceforth that education shall not be confined to a few, but shall be so diffused that there may not be a village with an ignorant family, nor a family with an ignorant member. Learning is no longer to be considered as belonging to the upper classes, but is to be equally the inheritance of nobles and gentry, farmers and artisans, males and females.

"For the purposes of administration it is directed that the whole empire, excepting the island of Yezo, which has a distinct colonial government, shall be divided into eight grand-school districts. The two cities of Tokio and Osaka, and the six provincial capitals, Aichi, Ishikawa, Hiroshima, Nagasaki, Niigata, and Awomori, have been designated as the seats for the establishment of colleges, and other important educational institutions. Each grand-school district is to be divided into thirty-two middle-school districts, in each of which a middle school will be established. Each middle-school district will be divided into elementary-school districts, and schools provided for each. Superintendents and inspectors are to be appointed, whose duty it will be to direct in regard to school-buildings, the organization of schools, and the management of moneys appropriated for school purposes."

Certain changes were found necessary in this plan of school administration. The number of grand-school districts was reduced to seven instead of eight. The number of middle-school districts has not been maintained at the designated figure. And in the settlement and establishment of elementary-school districts more attention has been given to the natural boundaries and association of communities than was originally deemed necessary. In the practical carrying out of all the plans there has been no hesitation in departing from the original schedule when circumstances required.

Schedules for Elementary and Higher Schools.—The department issued a scheme for the studies of the elementary schools. They were to be divided into two divisions, a junior division and a senior division; children of both sexes, from six to nine years of age, to compose the junior division, and those from ten to thirteen the senior division. The entire course was fixed at eight years. The subjects of instruction were reading and writing the Japanese language, arithmetic foreign and Japanese, geography, drawing, the elements of physics, chemistry, geometry, and history, together with drawing and the explanation of common things.

The middle schools were also divided into junior and senior divisions, and the course of study continued through six years. For entrance, the course of the elementary schools was required to have been finished. Besides the subjects of study of the elementary course which were here to be continued, the pupils were to be also taught a higher knowledge of the Japanese language together with some foreign language and such studies as ethics, political science, surveying, etc.

In this code of education were also prescribed regulations for the organization and management of foreign-language schools, and for university and technical courses of study to be pursued in the higher institutions for which provision was made. Rules for those studying in foreign countries were also laid down. The allowances for educational purposes to the different cities and provinces of the empire were settled. These regulations and the prescribed schedule of studies have been followed with only such modifications as the changing circumstances of the country made necessary.

Tokio Public Library.—In the eighth month of this year the Department of Education opened a public library. It was divided into two sections. In one were placed rare books, which were carefully guarded and preserved, and in the other common works intended for the use of the public. At first this library contained only Japanese and Chinese works, but in the year 1875 a large addition was made of foreign works. It is now kept in the old Temple of Confucius, which belonged to the College of Confucius, established under the shoguns.

The library is free to the public, and contains a valuable collection of native and foreign books as well as newspapers and other periodicals. In this month also the Department of Education was removed from its quarters in the old Confucian College to a building near the Kanda Bridge. The building vacated was turned over to the Normal School, which had previously been organized, but was now first opened for instruction. An office was also opened in connection with the Normal School for the preparation of school-books. Many of the school-charts and elementary text-books which are now used in the schools were prepared at this office.

In the eleventh month it was enacted that the old lunar calendar, which up to this time had been used in Japan, should be abolished, and in its place the Gregorian system should be substituted. Some confusion has arisen from this important change. Some of the old national holidays and festivals which, from time immemorial, had fallen upon certain dates according to the old calendar, were quite displaced by the new calendar. To this day some of these festivals are celebrated on two different days, according to the conservative or progressive views of different sections.

At the opening of the sixth year of Meiji (A. D. 1873), a government hospital was opened in the city of Tokio. To assist in defraying the expense of this establishment the Department of the Imperial Household made it a special grant of ten thousand yens, and the imperial court physicians were directed to give their services to it on their days of leave.

In the fourth month the eight grand-school districts which had been established in the code of education were consolidated into seven, and the number and boundaries of the elementary and middle school districts were readjusted. The proposed establishment of a college at Ishikawa Ken was abandoned, and Miyagi was substituted for Awamori as the proposed site of a college in the sixth grand-school district.

Development of the Institutions at Tokio.—It was at this time also that a new step in advance was taken in the development of the Foreign-

Language School in Tokio. A considerable number of the pupils had by this time advanced sufficiently far in their studies to enter upon those of a collegiate and technical character. It was, therefore, determined to set off from the Foreign-Language School those students sufficiently advanced for this purpose. From this time, therefore, may be dated the regular organization of a foreign college in Japan. The students still remaining in the Foreign-Language School continued to make the study of language and the preparatory branches of learning their chief occupation, while those set apart composed a newer organization under a separate director and with separate professors.

The Medical College, in like manner, was reorganized to meet the wants of the advanced condition of its students. A department was organized for the study of anatomy and other branches of medical science, while the students of the preparatory department were engaged in the study of foreign languages and elementary science.

A new building had been erected for the use of the Kaisei Gakko, by which name the new institution set off from the Foreign-Language School was designated. The old buildings were now occupied entirely by the classes of the Foreign-Language School. The opening of the new institution was signalized by a visit from the emperor in person accompanied by a number of the high officers of the Government; and a little later the empress also visited the institution, and personally inspected the operations of the different departments.

At this time, in the Foreign-Language School, English, French, German, Russian, and Chinese, were taught. The intercourse of Japan with the leading foreign nations made necessary the instruction of young men in these languages. In the Kaisei Gakko, three foreign languages were employed, English, French, and German. Subsequently, however, the use of one foreign language only was deemed essential to the economy and efficiency of the administration, and at the present time English alone is employed.

Additional Normal and Foreign-Language Schools.—The reorganization of the elementary schools had been especially aimed at in the code of education; and, although the provincial governments and the communities themselves were anxious for the improvement of their schools, and contributed willingly and liberally for this purpose, the want of competent teachers made it impossible to secure this object at once. To hasten the realization of this object, the Department of Education resolved to increase the number of normal schools, and in the ninth month directed the establishment of one at Osaka. In the early part of the next year they also organized normal schools at the towns of Aichi, Hiroshima, Nagasaki, and Niigata. This completed the provision of a normal school for each of the grand-school districts. They were all regulated upon the same plan and with the same subjects of study as the one already successfully begun in Tokio.

In the seventh year of Meiji (A. D. 1874) foreign-language schools were established in each of the grand-school districts, except in the first and second, where they already existed. They were located in the same towns where the normal schools were situated, to wit, at Tokio, Osaka, Hiroshima, Nagasaki, Miyagi, and Niigata. These foreign-language schools, with the exception of that at Tokio, were exclusively employed in teaching the English language, so that subsequently they were denominated English-language schools. The institution at Tokio was in the following year divided into two parts, the one called the English-Language School, and the other the Foreign-Language School.

Classification of Schools.—The educational institutions had now been brought into the condition in which they have since continued. They consisted of three classes: 1. Those which were established at the government expense, and maintained by a yearly allowance granted by the Department of Education, such as the Kaisei Gakko and Medical College in Tokio, the foreign-language schools and the normal schools in each of the grand-school districts. 2. Those which were built at the expense of the people, and were supported by the people, but received from the Department of Education a certain sum to assist in defraying their current expenses. These schools were under the supervision of the local governments, but were visited and inspected by the agents of the department. 3. Private schools, which were established by private individuals at their own expense. They were only required to report their regulations to the local government, and obtain a license.

In this year also the Department of Education began the publication of a semi-monthly bulletin, in which useful information on educational affairs and instructive discourses in regard to schools and sanitary matters were printed for the benefit of the public.

First Report presented to the Emperor.—In the first month of the eighth year of Meiji (A. D. 1875), on the anniversary of the day on which the Department of Education was organized, Tanaka Fujimaro, the vice-minister, presented the following address to the emperor:

"Your humble servant has had the good fortune to hold his office at a favorable time when civilization is beginning to be diffused, and the people are gradually becoming cultivated. Although it is my earnest desire to advance the affairs of this department, still it is not long since it was organized, and its operations are comparatively recent. In regard to sanitary matters which are at present under its direction its imperfection is apparent. But, in regard to its educational duties, it is the humble opinion of your servant that it has in some degree established order and system. I am, therefore, happy respectfully to present to your majesty the first annual report of this department. In this report for the sixth year of Meiji (A. D. 1874) are shown the internal arrangements of the department, together with the work it has accomplished, and the condition of the schools and school-districts regularly classified under appropriate heads. For the purpose of easy reference, an abridgment is attached. Owing to the necessity of respecting local customs, and to the incompleteness of the reports received from the cities and provinces, some discrepancies will be discovered. It is the opinion of your humble servant that the time when complete and correct reports may be obtained, and when such reports shall show that every family is educated and every individual is in good health, can only be reached by gradual and slow approximations. Your humble servant, therefore, respectfully presents this report, such as it is, and begs your majesty's gracious acceptance and examination of the same."

Female Normal School.—The most important event in educational matters of the year 1875 was the establishment of a female normal school. It is designed to train female teachers especially for the work of teaching in the elementary schools. The empress made a generous grant of five thousand yens toward this object. The building was completed in due time, and in the tenth month it was opened with appropriate ceremonies in the presence of the empress.

The Bureaus of Sanitary Affairs and of Press Regulations were during the year transferred from the Department of Education to the Department of Home Affairs, under which they are now managed.

CHAPTER V.

JAPANESE LANGUAGE AND LEARNING.

Origin of Japanese Written Characters.—In the earliest times the Japanese language had no written characters. The opinion entertained by some, that writing was known at the remotest times, has sprung from the belief that "Hifuma," "Anaichi," and "Hozuma" (mere forgeries of literary impostors), are really of ancient origin. In "Kogoshui," a collection of ancient traditions, Imube Hironari, its author, says, "In the remotest periods there were no written characters." This wellknown statement is most worthy of belief; for the author was a member of a family that during successive reigns was distinguished for talent and learning. He of all men should have known whether any characters had ever existed previous to those now in use; and, even supposing that such characters had once existed, whether they had been afterward lost. There is no doubt that, in the remotest periods, events were transmitted from mouth to mouth, without being reduced to writing, as is seen in the case of a history of Japan in three volumes, by Hiyetano Are, the contents of which, it appears, were recited and learned by heart before being reduced to writing. It is true that even before the end of the second century (European) many foreigners had come over to Japan from the continent; but we have no account of the introduction of Chinese or other characters at that early period. After the military expedition to Shinra, a part of Corea, the intercourse between that country and ours became more frequent—a circumstance which furnished reason to believe that some foreign characters were then introduced into the country; but we have no accounts of their having been then learned or used by the Japanese.

In the fifteenth year of the Emperor Ojin's reign (A. D. 284), the

King of Kudara, a part of Corea, sent a person called Ajiki to Japan, who was a good Confucian scholar. By this man the crown-prince Uji Wakairatsuko was taught to read the books of the sage. This is the first account we have of the introduction of Confucian books into our country. It appears that from that time sufficient progress was made in the study of letters to make epistolary correspondence practicable; but the writing of anything like Chinese composition was out of the question as yet. In "Kojiki," a history of Japan, and "Manyoshu," a collection of Japanese poetry, Chinese characters were indeed used, but only as phonetics of the Japanese sounds. As the square and unabbreviated form of the Chinese characters, however, consisted of so great a number of strokes as to occasion much perplexity, contractions and abbreviations were made; and so, after many and probably gradual changes, the characters assumed a permanent form called *Hirakana*, more or less different from the original. In some other characters, a part only of the original was retained, leaving out the more complicated part of the original, for the sake of convenience in writing. These abbreviated characters, being very simple, soon assumed a permanent form. Such was the origin of *Katakana*, or side-letters.

The popular opinion is, that the Hirakana, or plain letters, were invented by Kukai, while the Katakana, or side-letters, originated with Kibinomabi; but there is no sufficient proof in support of this opinion, and it probably arose from the natural tendency to attribute to particular individuals what was the result of general causes.

The table which stands below represents the syllabic sounds of the Japanese language, written in Katakana. By the combination of these, and a supplementary character corresponding to n, always placed at the end of a syllable, all the words of the Japanese language may be represented:

AN OUTLINE HISTORY OF

THE JAPANESE SYLLABARY.[1]

ワ	ラ	ヤ	マ	ハ	ナ	タ	サ	カ	ア
wa	ra	ya	ma	ha	na	ta	sa	ka	a
井	リ	イ	ベ	ヒ	ニ	チ	シ	キ	イ
wi	ri	yi	mi	hi	ni	tsi	shi	ki	i
ウ	ル	ユ	ム	フ	ヌ	ツ	ス	ク	ウ
wu	ru	yu	mu	fu	nu	tsu	su	ku	u
ヱ	レ	エ	メ	ヘ	子	テ	セ	ケ	エ
we	re	ye	me	he	ne	te	se	ke	e
ヲ	ロ	ヨ	モ	ホ	ノ	ト	ソ	コ	オ
wo	ro	yo	mo	ho	no	to	so	ko	o

The origin of this syllabary is unknown, but we think we are justified in supposing that it dated from the return of Kukai, the Buddhist priest, from China, and the introduction of Sanskrit by him. For, though there is some difference of opinion on this point, yet the arrangement of the syllables adopted by the best authorities is the order corresponding to the vowel-sounds (*a, i, u, e, o*); and this order is derived from the five vowel-sounds in the ancient Hindostani writing—a feature which we do not find to exist in the syllabaries of any other language. When Kukai went over to China, he was instructed by Fukuzanzo in the ancient Hindostani writing and the sounds of the Hindostani characters. These branches of learning were entirely neg-

---

[1] In giving the equivalent sounds in Roman characters, we have followed the system now adopted by most Anglo-Japanese scholars. The sounds of the consonants are the same as in English, and the sounds of the vowels the same as in Italian. The table is to be read in vertical columns, beginning at the right hand.

lected in China toward the latter part of the Gen dynasty; but with us, especially by the numerous Shingon sect, which was founded by Kukai, they continued to be extensively and attentively cultivated. It is, therefore, tolerably certain that Buddhist priests composed the table of fifty syllables. What the gamut is to vocal harmony, this table is to prosody and to the art of combining initial and final sounds by means of characters. But, there being but forty-seven syllables in our language, the table contains a few supernumerary ones. There are in the table, too, slight inconsistencies; but, on the whole, the classification of the syllables is clear and the sounds are well harmonized. On account of its simplicity and convenience, the table is now very generally used by scholars.

But, besides the above usual arrangement of the syllabary, other arrangements have been used: for instance, we also have *a, e, o, u, i,* or, *u, o, i, e, a,* instead of *a, i, u, e, o,* and, instead of the common lateral order, these two modified systems respectively follow the order of *a, wa, ya, na, ta, ra, ha, ma, ka, sa,* and *a, ra, ma, wa, ka, sa, ta, na, ha, ya,* and these kana are therefore placed at the head of the ten columns of syllables in the tables, to indicate the modified lateral order of the columns in those peculiar arrangements.

Some recent writers say that this table of syllables was invented by sages of the remotest ages for the use of the people, or that it was made by the sacred kings in ancient Hindostan; but both these statements are forced inferences drawn from the fact that it is now extensively used. The nicely-harmonized system of the syllabary, as it stands in the table of fifty sounds, appears to be of divine origin. In the foregoing table of the Japanese syllabary, we have fifty syllables arranged in regular order; but our language has in reality no more than forty-seven. It will be seen that in the column *ya, yi, yu, ye, yo,* the characters for *yi* and *ye* do not differ from those for *i* and *e;* and in that of *wa, wi, wu, we, wo,* the character for *wu* is the same as that for *u.*

There is another arrangement of the Japanese syllabary said to have been invented by the priest Kobodaishi, who was one of the most celebrated Japanese scholars. It was contrived for the purpose of facilitating the memorizing of the syllabary. Being divided into words the whole composes the following celebrated stanza :

> I-ro-ha ni-ho-he-to chi-ri-nu-ru-wo
> Wa-ga-yo ta-re-so tsu-ne-ra-n
> Wi-no-o-ku ya-ma ke-fu-ko-ye-te
> A-sa-ki yu-me mi-shi e-hi-se-su.

From the first three letters in this arrangement the syllabary is commonly called the *I-ro-ha*, just as the English word *alphabet* has been derived from the first two Greek letters.

Written Characters of the Legendary Age.—We have said above that the so-called characters of the legendary age were not made by the sages of old. But the opinion entertained by some writers, that they were derived from the Corean Rito (a system of writing), is not supported by facts. According to our opinion, these characters are identical with those known as "new characters," and were extant at our Board of Books and Writings during the middle ages.

In the eleventh year of the reign of the Emperor Temmu (A. D. 683) these new characters were made by Sakaibe-no-Muraji Iwasumi by imperial command; but they were never generally used in Japan. Shimbun was King of Shinra (part of Corea), and, an irregular intercourse having sprung up with that country, I am convinced that these characters were then introduced into Corea, for at the present time they are called vulgar characters by the Coreans, and are in general use with them. The composition of the table has by them been attributed to Setsuso, a distinguished scholar of that early time.

But, while we have the square and unabbreviated, as well as the cursive form of these characters, they have only the former without the latter, which latter form I think was never introduced into Corea. Of both forms of characters, some specimens are extant in the old Shinto temples of our country. This is probably owing to the fact that the use of the Chinese characters did not spread so early and so extensively in the country as it did in the cities and towns. The "new characters" were known and used until the middle ages, and were called Satsujin and Hijin characters (i. e., characters used by the people of Satsuma, and Hizen, and Higo).

Such is our opinion concerning those characters which Hirata Atsutane, the most distinguished scholar of recent times, held to be the oldest Japanese characters, and which Ban Nobutomo pronounced to be purely Corean. These two opinions, however, are not free from doubt, and I therefore set forth my opinion, committing the question to the future examination of others.

Pure Japanese Characters.—As said above, in the remotest periods of our country, we had no written characters; but, in later times, several new characters have been invented here. The characters have forms similar to the Chinese; but are not contained in Chinese dictionaries, because they are of purely Japanese origin.

There are also some Chinese characters which have been generally used here, but, having become extinct in China, are said by some to be of Japanese origin. Such characters have been attributed to Japanese invention erroneously, on account of their absence in Chinese dictionaries. Besides the above, some Chinese characters have been naturalized here in a corrupt form, and have become Japanese. A few dictionaries which contain characters of the above classes are still extant:

Wamiyorui-jusho, a dictionary, composed about A. D. 900.

Ruiju-meigi-sho, a dictionary, composed about A. D. 900.

Shin-sen-jikio, a dictionary, composed about A. D. 900.

Shin-sen-sarugakuki, a work compiled about A. D. 1080.

Iroha-jiruisho, a work written about A. D. 1500.

Wagiyokûhen, a work written about the same time.

Unpô-iroha-sho, a work written about the same time.

Teikinorai, a work written about A. D. 1320.

Isei-teikin, a work written A. D. 1330.

Sekiso-orai, a work written A. D. 1450.

Shinsen-ruiju-orai, a work written about A. D. 1500.

Kagaku-shu, a work written about the same time.

Setsuyo-shu, of which an edition, called Soji, was published about A. D. 1500, and another, called Yekirin, was published about A. D. 1600.

The characters in question mentioned in the above works are too numerous to be repeated here.

The Table of Marks.—In order to render Chinese writing intelligible to a Japanese reader, without making a complete translation, certain marks are fixed to the Chinese text, to indicate the order in which the Chinese characters must be read to suit the Japanese idiom. Some particles too are inserted at the side of the Chinese characters to show the relation of words to each other. These supplementary elements have collectively been called "The Tables of Marks." The use of these tables was well defined previous to the middle ages, and was designed to secure the correct rendering of Chinese texts. But in modern times the free and arbitrary use of those marks has frequently given rise to a misunderstanding of the sense of the composition to which they were affixed ; and, what is still worse, sometimes serious errors were created, by attributing ideas to an author which he had neither entertained nor expressed. We quote from Dr. Hepburn's article on "The Japanese Language," in Appletons' "American Cyclopædia," his statement in regard to the use of the Chinese characters in Japanese literature : "There are three general styles of literary composition in use. One is pure Chinese, in which none but Chinese characters are employed, and the grammatical construction is in accordance with the Chinese idiom. Frequently, in this style, marks or signs are used along the line of the characters to designate the order in which they should be read in translating the sentences into the Japanese language, or to suit the native idiom. Another, and the most common, is that in which the Chinese characters are used to a greater or less extent, mixed with native words written with their own letters, and where the structure and idiom are purely Japanese. Most of the literature intended for the unlearned and common reader is in this form. There is still another, written almost entirely in the native character, with little or no admixture of Chinese, intended for the use of women and children and uneducated persons."

COMPOSITION.

In very ancient times, as already related, writing was unknown, and oral language only existed. From such records as are left of this language, we know that its form was graceful, its sound harmonious, and its style rich in ornament; but, owing to the non-existence of letters to preserve it, only a very small portion has descended to our times, as for instance, in the Koden (ancient records), Notto (Shinto prayers), etc. And we owe the preservation of even this small amount to the fact that the " Koden " were orally taught from generation to generation, and the " Notto " were particular forms of prayer used from age to age on religious festivals. In such works as " Kojiki," " Fudoki," etc., we find analogical sentences joined together in couplets, which give us some idea of the style of this ancient language.

When the emperor issued proclamations upon any important state business, they were called Sen-miyo. They were written in large characters; grammatical inflections, etc., being expressed by the aid of small auxiliary characters inserted between the larger ones. It is only these Sen-miyo and Notto that are exclusively or purely Japanese. Even in modern times this style is used in religious festivals, the naming of an heir to the crown, the imperial marriage, the changing of the year's name, the appointing of ministers, etc. From the close of the sixth century of the Christian era, Chinese compositions began to be studied, and, as in all things Chinese customs were respected, the ordinary writing became entirely Chinese; on this account, even in the above-mentioned Sen-miyo, a few Chinese words found entrance. In this way the documents issued by the Government gradually came to be written in Chinese. From about A. D. 900, students ceased to go to China to study, and. communication with that country becoming infrequent, Chinese grammar became corrupted, and the result was that a hybrid style of composition was created by this confusion. This is the style now used by the Government in its documents, and by the people in their daily correspondence. In this style the characters On and Soro are indiscriminately used to express respect. Although this is the style currently used, there is another style which sprung from the most ancient forms, and became a style distinct by itself. It had its origin in the Japanese middle ages, at about the period of Yengi (A. D. 901-922). The works "Tosa Nikki," etc., by Kino Tsurayuki, were written in this style. Before the issue of this work, indeed, the works "Isemonogatari," "Taki-torimono-gatari," etc., existed; but the "Tosa Nikki" is the oldest work concerning whose authorship no doubt exists. The styles Sho-soku-bun (Japanese epistolary style), Wakanojo (style for introductions to Japanese practical works), Nikki and Kiko (diaries and travels), and Monogatari (light literature), sprung out of the above-mentioned mediæval style.

Nikki and Kiko Style.—Between this style and the Monogatari style there exists but little difference. The use of honorific terms, as in the Sho-soku-bun, did not prevail when this style was in vogue. It is noted for its plainness and *naïveté;* in fact, it represents things as they are. At least, these were its peculiarities from A. D. 900 to A. D. 1000, after which, however, it gradually was encumbered with ornaments, so that at length it was merged in the Monogatari style.

Monogatari Style.—Its simplest form is seen in the "Take-tori Monogatari," and the height of its elegance appears in the "Genji Monogatari. The former is of about A. D. 900, the latter of about A. D. 1000; which accounts for the increased elegance of this style.

Waka-no-jo Style.—There was a peculiar style of composition used for precursive remarks to poetical stanzas; this style was also employed in writing the epilogistic remarks to a verse. These remarks often served the double purpose of sequel to the stanza it followed, and of preface to the one it preceded. This style belonged to the Waka-no-jo.

It was also used in writing short introductions to poetical works; and again it was used when people assembled together for the purpose of composing verses. These verses, when collected, were preceded by an introduction explanatory of the special occasion of such assembly, written in this style, with richly-ornamental flourishes. This highly-ornamented style is derived from that used in the introductions to Chinese poetical works, and prevailed in the later mediæval times, about A. D. 1000; but it is only a modified form of Chinese composition, with mere addition of rhetorical flourishes.

Metrical Composition.—Poetry has existed from the most ancient times, and, as it was handed down from generation to generation by word of mouth, even now some of the oldest poetry is extant. Poetry or song is generally understood to be delivered in audible intoned cadence; but, since the middle ages (Japanese), poetry has been divided into two kinds, the one being simply read, while the other kind is sung. The latter kind consisted of Kagura, Saibaraku, Imaiyo, Yo-kiyoku, etc., while the former developed into a distinct subject of literary art. There were two kinds of verse, one of five syllables and one of seven syllables. Verses, however, of six and eight syllables were also composed. Although there were no fixed rules for the length of the stanzas, still in more modern times the usual rule was that they should be of thirty-one syllables. But as yet poetry had not developed into a distinct art. It first became so during the period of Choho (A. D. 999-1003), when the Buddhist priest No-in became the pupil of Fujiwara Nagato, and Fujiwara Toshinari became the pupil of Fujiwara Mototoshi. With these, during the later mediæval age, originated the peculiar style of Nijo, Beizen, and Asukai (these are family names), and these styles were followed by everybody. But in later ages, these styles having been found to be erroneous, the Buddhist priests Keichiu, Kamo Mabuchi, etc., purified them, and remodeled them so as to be conformable to the ancient style. Fujitani Nariakira, of Kioto, classified the various styles of poetry according to six periods, which he called 1. Josei (ancient period); 2. Chiuko (early mediæval period); 3. Nakagoro (mediæval period); 4. Kinko (later mediæval period); 5. Kinsei (modern period); 6. Konsei (present period). Examples of the styles of these periods are here appended:

I. Josei (Ancient Period).

Ya-ku-mo-ta-tsu.................................... (5)
I-dsu-mo ya-ye ga-ki............................... (7)
Tsu-ma-go-mi ni................................... (5)
Ya-ye ga-ki tsu-ku-ru.............................. (7)
So-no ya-ye ga-ki wo............................... (7)
    By Su-sa no-no mi-ko-to.

Ta-ta na-me-te... (5)
I-na-sa no-ya-ma-no....................................... (7)
Ko-no ma yo mo.. (5)
I-yu-ki ma-mo-rahi... (7)
Ta-ta-ka-he-ba... (5)
Wa-re ha-ya we-nu... (6)
Shi-ma-tsu do-ri.. (5)
U-ka-hi ga to mo... (6)
I-ma-su ke ni ko-ne.. (7)
    By Jimmu Tenno.

II. CHIUKO (Early Mediæval Period).

The style of this period first came into vogue about A. D. 850, and was at its height about A. D. 900.

EXAMPLES OF ITS EARLIER AGE.

I-to to si-ku... (5)
Su-gi-yu-ku ka-ta no....................................... (7)
Ko-hi-si-ki ni.. (5)
U-ra-ya-ma si-ku-mo....................................... (7)
Ka-he-ru na-mi-ka-na...................................... (7)

It flourished most during the periods Yengi (A. D. 901–922) and Tenriyaku (A. D. 947–956). There being eminent poets at this time, poetical assemblies were held even at the imperial court; and, this art being generally cultivated, the style was extremely good.

Sa-ku-ra ba-na... (5)
Sa-ki ni ke-ra-si na.. (7)
A-si-bi-ki no... (5)
Ya-ma-no ka-hi ya-ri....................................... (7)
Mi-yu-ru si-ra-ku-mo....................................... (7)

To-si-fu-re-ba... (5)
Ko-si-no si-ra ya-ma....................................... (7)
O-yi ni ke-ri.. (5)
O ho-ku no to-si no.. (7)
Yu-ki tsu-mo-ri tsu-tsu..................................... (7)

III. AND IV. CHIUSEI (Mediæval Period).

This period is subdivided into Nakagoro and Kinko (mediæval and later mediæval periods). The former is distinguished for the solidity, the latter for the floridness and elegance of its style. This latter style came into vogue about A. D. 1100.

EXAMPLES OF STYLE OF NAKAGORO.

Ha-ru-sa me ni.. (5)
Nu-re-te ta dzu-nem .... (7)
Ya-ma za-ku-ra... (5)
Ku-mo no ka he si no... (7)
A-ra-si mo zo fu-ku... (7)

EXAMPLES OF THE STYLE OF KINKO.

Yo no na-ka ha.. (5)
Wa-ga mi ni so-he-ru.. (7)
Ka-ge na-re ya.. (5)
O-mo-hi su-tsu-re-do.. (7)
Ha-na-re-za-ri ke-ri... (7)

Ta-dzu-ne ki-te... (5)
Ha-na-ni ku-ra-se-ru.. (7)
Ko-no ma yo-ri.. (5)
Ma-tsu to-si mo na-ki... (7)
Ya-ma no ha no tsu-ki... (7)

Fu-ru sa-to ni.. (5)
Ki-ki si a-ra-si no... (7)
Ko-we mo ni zo.. (5)
Wa-su-re-ne hi-to wo.. (7)
Sa-ya no na-ka-ya-ma.. (7)

V. KINSEI (Modern Period).

This also is subdivided into two periods; the first flourished before the period Bun-po (A. D. 1317–1318), and the other about the period Yekiyo (A. D. 1429–1440.)

EXAMPLES.

Fu-ke nu-re-ba... (5)
U-ra mim to da ni.. (7)
O-mo-fu ma-ni.. (5)
Ko-nu-yo si-ra-ru-ru....................................... (7)
To-ri no ko-we ka-na....................................... (7)

Although in this we perceive a decline of force and power, still in elegance and grace great improvements are visible.

VI. KONSEI (Present Period.)

Although the best pieces of this period are in imitation of the Kinsei, still they have peculiarities of their own which entitle them to a separate classification. The compositions of about A. D. 1500 almost all belong to this period. About A. D. 1700 the ancient style was revived; the poetry after this date, therefore, resembles that of ancient times.

EXAMPLES.

Se-ki no na-no... (5)
Ka-su-mi mo tsu-ra si...................................... (7)
Ka-he-ri mi-ru... (5)
Ki-no-hu-no so-ra mo....................................... (7)
Ke-hu-ha he-da-te-te....................................... (7)

Chinese Composition (*Kambun*).—The introduction of Chinese composition into Japan took place during the reign of the Emperor Ojin (A. D. 270–312); but what the style of this composition was at this age it is impossible to say. In the fourth year of the reign of the Empress Suiko (A. D. 596), at Dogo, in the province of Iyo, a stone monument was erected, and, although this monument no longer exists, still a copy of the inscription which was engraved upon it is preserved in the work "Shaku Nihonki." Thirty-one years after this, an image of Buddha was made, upon the back of which an inscription was engraved; and, although this idol yet exists in the temple of Hori-uji of Yamato, still, owing to the Japanese not yet having obtained perfection in Chinese composition, and also to the fact that the inscription has been partially effaced by time, there are portions of it which it is impossible to read.

About eighty or ninety years later, Futo Yasumaro presented to the emperor the work "Kojiki" (Japanese ancient history), and he prefaced it with an address to the emperor composed in pure Chinese, which was very different from the two inscriptions mentioned above. After this, Chinese came over to Japan, and Japanese students went to China. For a time Chinese composition was extensively used; but afterward, since about A. D. 900, intercourse with China ceased, and no more students went to that country, so that finally a peculiar Japanese style of Chinese composition arose, in which the characters were not read in the same order as they were written. Those coming first in order when writing a sentence being placed at the end of the sentence in reading; the characters forming no complete meaning if read as they were written. This hybrid style is in use at the present time for epistolary correspondence and for government documents.

In ancient times, neither literary studies nor books for imparting knowledge existed in this country. It was only subsequent to the middle ages that the study of history and of ancient customs was commenced, and this was confined to the members of the imperial court only, the mass of the people not occupying themselves with these matters, nor with the imperial records on local customs and usages which were composed about this time. In the eighth month of the fourth year of the reign of the Emperor Richiu (A. D. 403), offices were first established in the provinces for the purpose of recording local events, public opinions, etc., but before this a similar office existed in the imperial court. Afterward, during the reign of the Empress Suiko (A. D. 595–628), the following works were composed: "Tennoki" (historical record of the successive emperors), "Kokuki" (provincial records), and chronicles of the two families of Omi and Muraji; but in the fourth year of the reign of the Empress Kokiyoku (A.D. 645), during the feud with Iruka and Emiji, these works were burnt. Later, in the fifth year of Dado (A.D. 712), during the reign of the Empress Gemmiyo, Futo Yasumaro presented her with a history which he had composed from the personal narrative of the Emperor Temmu, and still later the six histories, "Nihon-shoki," "Buntoku-jitsuroku," and "Sandai-jitsuroku," were successively written. But they were written in Chinese, so that without explanation the unlettered could not understand them. Hence there existed in the middle ages rules for the interpretation of the Nihonki, and gradually it came to be considered as a religious work on Shintoism. Both Shinto and Buddhist priests explained it as a work on Confucianism or Buddhism, so that at last incorrect opinions and statements were formed, with which the ignorant were misled. Owing to the frequent wars, however, these doctrines were neglected, and at last there were none who believed in them. In the period of Genroku (A.D. 1688-1703), the Buddhist priest Keichiu, of the province of Settsu, who was clever in composing Japanese poetry, in order to acquire a knowledge of old Japanese words, consulted all kinds of books, so that eventually he corrected the erroneous opinions of the scholars of the middle ages, and the true meaning of old Japanese was in some degree made clear. Contemporaneous with Keichiu, the Shinto priest Hagura Itsuki, of Yamashiro, calling himself Kada Adzumamaro, carefully examined old works, and discovered much in them; and one of his pupils, Okabe Yeji, of Totomi, who also called himself Kamo no Mabuchi, corrected many errors of long standing. He was the first to excite a general interest in the cultivation of Japanese learning, and to him is due the revival of the study of Shinto sacred works, history, poetry, etc. Moto-ori Nobunaga, of the province of Ise, one of his scholars, found out much that his master had not discovered, and recovered a considerable store of historical, antique, and poetic knowledge, that had been lost for more than a thousand years, thus greatly increasing and stimulating learning. This learning was called "*Japanese* learning," in distinction from Chinese learning.

Among his pupils were Murata Harumi and Kato Chikage. The former was noted for his acquaintance with law and ancient customs; the latter was well versed in poetic lore, and was also expert in composing poetry. After this there were many who applied themselves to Japanese learning, but there were none who were not indebted to the abovementioned scholars, and to them is also due the universal prevalence, at the present day, of "Japanese learning" in the empire.

Confucian Learning (*Jugaku*).—The origin of Confucian learning dates from the fifteenth year of the reign of the Emperor Ojin (A. D. 284), when Ajiki came from Kudara, in Corea, and taught the imperial Prince Uji Wakai-iratsuko the Chinese classics. In the following year Wani came to Japan and became the prince's teacher. This was the source from which Confucian learning originated, and gradually increased and spread. In the seventh year of the Emperor Keitai (A. D. 513), Danyoji came over from Corea, and in the tenth year of the same reign Ko-ammo followed. After this others came over and taught, while students went from Japan to Corea to study. In the first year of the reign of the Emperor Kotoku (A. D. 645), the Buddhist priest Bin and Takamuku Kuromasa were appointed professors of Confucian learning. In the seventh year of the reign of the Empress Suiko, A. D. 599, they had returned to Japan from their studies abroad. By imperial command, in the second year of the same reign, eight government departments and a hundred offices were organized under the direction of these two professors, and it is probable that at this time a university was also established. At a later time, the mode of examination was made the same as it was in China. We may, therefore, conclude that at this time there were many learned scholars.

After the middle ages the two families of Kiyowara and Nakahara were intrusted with the direction of the study of the Chinese classics, while the families of Sugawara and Oye were concerned principally with Chinese composition. Subsequently students ceased to go abroad, and foreigners ceased to come over. Moreover, continual wars raged, and learning fell entirely into the hands of the Buddhist priesthood. In the period of Tensho (A. D. 1573–1591), Soshun, the second son of the noble Reizen Tamezumi, became a priest of the Buddhist temple Sokokuji. Having studied the works of the philosophers Tei and Shu, being the first who did so, he left the priesthood, called himself Fujiwara Shiku, and also took the surname Seikwa. Hayashi Doshun, Matsunaga Sekigo, Nawa Doin, and others, were among his pupils. After this Chinese learning once more began to flourish, and supporters of the doctrines of Yomei arose, while others devoted themselves to the study of the art of composing by the aid of ancient Chinese characters. In consequence of this, the descendants of old families such as Sugawara, Kiyowara, and others, at this time became learned scholars.

Schools (Gakko).—The first mention of a school-director (Fumiya-no-kami, i. e., commissioner of schools) is made in the tenth year of the reign of the Emperor Tenji (A. D. 664), when Kishitsu Shushin was invested with this rank. However, as the Buddhist priest Bin and Ta-kamuku Kuromasa were appointed professors in the first year of the reign of the Emperor Kotoku (A. D. 645), and in the fifth year of the same reign, the eight departments and one hundred offices were created; it is probable that at this time also a school was opened and a Fumiya-no-kami (commissioner of schools) was appointed. Afterward, in the fourth year of the reign of the Emperor Temmu (A. D. 676), the Daigaku Riyo (university department) existed, among the officers of which the several ranks of Kami (chief), Suki (vice-chief), Daijo (senior secretary), Shojo (junior secretary), Dai Sakan (senior clerk), and Sho-sakan (junior clerk), existed. These officers managed all matters connected with the university. For providing instruction a Hakase (professor) and two Jokiyo (assistant teachers) were appointed, who taught the classes. There were four hundred students, who were divided into various classes, each studying the subject taught in the class to which he belonged. Besides the above teachers, there were two On-Hakase (professors of the sounds of Chinese characters), two Sho-Hakase (writing-masters), and two San-Hakase (arithmeticians); these two last mentioned taught each thirty students. The above was the number of officers, teachers, and students, as fixed by law during the period of Taiho (A. D. 701-703). But, although this system was adhered to in after-times, some slight changes were made, such as the appointing and abolishing of Kiden-Hakase (professors of history and records) and Ritsugaku-Hakase (professors of law), and the addition of Bunsho-Hakase (professors of composition) and Meiho-Hakase (law professors). Excepting these slight changes, the before-mentioned system was adhered to.

In after-times the two families of Sugawara and Oye established in the university a bunsho-in (composition-school), which was divided into East Hall and West Hall, the chief of the former being Sugawara, while the latter was directed by Oye. Here composition was exclusively taught and encouraged. Although such was the condition of the university, still before the period of Genkiyo (A. D. 1321-1323) and Remmu (A. D. 1334-1335) it had gradually declined, and at last, after the wars of the period of Onin (A. D. 1467-1468), not even a trace of it remained.

Contemporaneously with the university at Kioto, schools existed and flourished in all the provinces. In each of these provincial schools there was a hakase (professor), a doctor (i. e., medical professor), etc. In the very large provinces the number of students was fifty; in the larger provinces it was forty; in those of medium size it was thirty; and in the smaller twenty. Those among these students who successfully passed the examinations of the Shikibu (Board of Rites) were admitted to the university. Although it is impossible to say when these provincial schools ceased to exist, yet, owing to the gradual breaking up of the local governments, and to the cessation of the old rule of sending chief magistrates from Kioto, the diffusion of education came to a standstill in every part of the empire.

Private Schools (Shigaku).—The establishment of private schools originated with the noble Wage Kiyomaro, whose son Hiroyo, carrying out and fulfilling his father's intentions, converted, during the period of Yenriyaku (A. D. 782-805), his own residence into a school, which he called the Kobun-in. Afterward the Kuangaku-in of the Fujiwara family, the Gak-kuan-in of the Tachibana family, and the Sogaku-in of the Ariwara family, were established. The Sogaku-in was founded by Ariwara Yukihira; the Gaku-kuan-in by Tachibana Kachiko, the imperial consort of the Emperor Saga (A. D. 850); and the Kuan-gaku-in by Fujiwara Fuyustugu. The use of each of these schools was confined to the members of the respective families who had founded them.

The first private school established by the military class was founded about the year A. D. 1215 or 1216, by Akitoki, the grandson of Hojo Yoshitoki, at Kanazawa, where he resided, and by which name he called himself. To this school he added a library, and collected books.

At the present day books bearing the stamp of the Kanazawa Library are to be found here and there; these books all belonged to this school. After this, during the prevalence of wars, it happened from time to time that the powerful chieftains who acquired dominions established schools for the benefit of the members of their families and of their retainers, but none of these reached the flourishing condition of the Shoheiko founded by the Tokugawa family.

The origin of this school was as follows: Dainagon Tokugawa Yoshinawo founded, at the country-seat of Hayashi Doshun, situated in Uyeno, a school which he called the Kobun-in. In the fourth year of Genroku (A. D. 1691) this school was removed by the Shogun Tokugawa Tsunayoshi to the ascent of Shohei, and here a magnificent temple in honor of Confucius was built, where the shogun's retainers received education. Rules for examination were fixed, and those who were found proficient were appointed to office. This was called the Shohei-zaka-gaku-monjo, and the festivals, etc., held in spring and autumn, in honor of Confucius, were very celebrated.

EXAMINATIONS AND CLASSIFICATION OF HONORS.

According to the book of laws, called Riyo, examinations were divided into the four classes of Shiu-sai, Meikei, Shin-shi, and Mei-ho. To these were added examinations in penmanship and mathematics, thus forming six subjects similar to the six examinations which had been established in China during the dynasty of To. The candidates for examination were divided into two kinds, namely, those sent from the university, who were called *Kiojin*, and those sent from the provinces, who were called *Kojin*. The following are the particulars of the above:

Shiu-sai.—The candidates for this examination were chosen from those who had read many books. Two important subjects were selected upon which essays were to be composed, such subjects, for instance, as the following : "What was the cause of the abundance of sages during the Chinese dynasty of Shu?"

Those whose composition was conspicuously elegant and pure, and whose reasoning was very acute and sound, received the rank of Jo-no-jo (First of the First). Those whose composition was equally good, but did not reach so high a standard in reason, received the rank of Jo-no-chiu (Medium of the First). Those who were noted for their reasoning, but less so for the style of their composition, took this degree also. Those whose composition and reasoning were only good, took the rank of Chiu-no-jo (First of the Medium). Those whose work was below this did not take any degree.

The Jo-no-jo received the honorary rank of Sho-hachi-i.

The Jo-no-chiu that of Sho-hachi-i-ge.

The others did not receive any rank, but were attached to the department of Shikibu, and when vacancies occurred they were filled from among them, and together with this appointment rank was conferred.

Mei-kei.—This examination consisted of one subject out of each of the Chinese classical works of "Shurai," "Sâden," "Raiki," and "Moshi," three other subjects from among the other Chinese classics, and also three subjects from the two Chinese classics of "Kokiyo" and "Rongo," in all ten subjects. In all these subjects questions were asked both upon the original text and the commentaries.

All those who clearly and correctly explained the sense of both the text and the commentaries passed. Those successfully passing in the ten subjects receiving the degree of Jo-no-jo; those passing in eight and more received the degree of Jo-no-chiu. Those who passed in six received the degree of Chiu-no-jo. Those who passed in only five subjects and one classic, and besides failed in Rongo and Kokiyo, obtained no degree, while those who comprehended two or more classics were examined in one subject selected from each of the classics, being required to give the principal ideas, and, if five or more subjects were successfully answered, the candidates passed. The Jo-no-jo received the rank of Sho-hachi-i-ge; the Jo-no-chiu that of Ju-hachi-i-jo; the others were rated the same as for the Shiu-sai examination.

Shin-shi.—This examination consisted of two subjects upon public matters of the period, seven trials of memory in reading the work "Monsen," and three in the work "Jiga." These trials were made by concealing certain characters, which characters were to be supplied in reading the passage.

Those who answered the two questions on public matters in a clear and correct manner, and successfully read the passage in which some character was concealed, obtained the degree of Ko.

Those who were successful in passing the questions, but failed in not more than four of the passages, took the degree of Otsu.

All others did not obtain any degree.

Meiho.—This consisted of seven questions on Ritsu (law), and three upon Riyo.

Those who answered correctly the two questions took the degree of Ko.

Those who failed in not more than two took the degree of Otsu.

Penmanship (Sho).—Those who formed and finished the characters with elegance passed.

Mathematics (San).—This examination consisted in three questions on the work "Kiusho," and one question in each of the works "Kaito," "Shiuhi," "Goso," "Kiushi," "Sonshi," "Sankai," and "Chosa."

Those who passed successfully in all took the degree of Ko.

Those who failed in not more than four took the degree of Otsu.

But, although six questions were successfully answered, still, if those on the Kiusho had not been answered, no degree was conferred.

Penmanship (Sho-gaku).—In this country the manner of writing was learned by copying Chinese writing, and in ancient ages did not differ from the Chinese; and, if we examine old records and manuscripts, we find that the character in which they are written is exactly similar to the Chinese.

In the period of Yen-riyaku (A. D. 947-956), Ono-no Tofu, a celebrated calligrapher, composed seventeen rules of penmanship; and, in the period of Kuan-jin (A. D. 1014-1020), Fujiwara Yukinari made sixteen different specimens of handwriting. From these two originated a kind of Wafuo (Japanese style). The style which these two introduced was, in later ages, called Jodairiu (ancient style). The Fushimi-in style also sprung out of the above-mentioned style. The Imperial Prince Sonyen, son of the Emperor Fushimi-in, afterward introduced the rich and beautiful style of Sonyenriu; this prince was the designer of the purest Japanese style. The Prince Sondo learned this style, and originated another style, which, in later times, was called Onye-riu (imperial style).

Until recent days a knowledge of this style of writing was necessary to be able to obtain a secretaryship under the government; on this account all writing-masters taught it to their pupils. Although this style generally prevailed, still gentlemen and poets occasionally introduced new styles, which they named after themselves; but in reality no great difference existed between them. Those, however, which were most readily recognized by their peculiarities were the Tei-ka, Konoye, Takimoto, and Royetsu styles.

The Chinese style of writing now in use was originated by Hosoi-Chishu. He was a native of Yedo, and adopted the name of Kotaku. His style was in great vogue during the period of Genroku (A. D. 1688-1703), being called the Karayo (Chinese style). Among his pupils was Matsushita Kasshin, who called himself Useki. He became, like his master, very celebrated for penmanship. Immediately succeeding these, Akai Tokusui, Toko Genriu, and others, attained to celebrity; nevertheless, the styles which became especially popular were the recent ones of Ichikawa Sangai and Maki Taijin. At present the Maki Taijin style is as universal as the Oye style formerly was.

CHAPTER VI.

JAPANESE ARTS AND SCIENCES.

Drawing and Painting (Ga-gaku).—Although Japanese pictures are not imitations of those of other countries, still the art was originally acquired from foreigners. The earliest mention made of foreign artists is in the seventh year of the reign of the Emperor Yuriyaku (A. D. 463), when, by imperial command, various artists were sent over from Kudara, in Corea, and among these was the painter Inshiraga. Though many other artists afterward came to this country, none of their authenticated productions remain. There exists, however, at the present day, in the temple of Horiuji, in the province of Yamato, portraits, etc., of the Imperial Prince Shotoku; these works have in all probability descended from that ancient period.

Subsequently, a painting-department was established in the government, to which, besides the managing officers, were attached four Gashi (artists) and sixty Gabu (inferior artists or sketchers). This department was probably created during the period of Taiho (A. D. 701-703). In the third year of Taido (A. D. 808), it was abolished as a distinct department, and was incorporated with the Takumi-riyo (architectural department), in which a Yedokoro (government studio) was formed, and to which a chief, styled Yedokoro-adzukari, was attached. Although this was the case, still it would appear that the principal purpose of this office was the decoration, etc., of the imperial palace; so that no great skill was at that time attained to in drawing and painting. But, after Koze Hirotaka became the Yedokoro-adzukari, this office was filled from age to age by skillful painters.

Besides, there were many private artists who were noted for their skill; such as Fujiwara Mototsune, Fujiwara Nobuzane, Sojoakuyu, and others. Their works are noted for clearness of outline and the minute and delicate handling of the details. Afterward the style gradually changed into one of less vigor but of greater beauty, and more particularly noted for the fineness of its strokes. The art was used to delineate court nobles in their dress of ceremony, and other similar subjects. The creations of this style were called Yamato or Tosa pictures; they received the latter appellation from Tsunetaka, the grandson of the Yedokoro-adzukari, Fujiwara Takayoshi. He became vice-governor of the province of Tosa, and hence his descendants adopted the family name of Tosa. Among these descendants was Hiromichi, who, in the second year of Kanbun (A. D. 1662), changed the family name to Sumiyoshi.

During the middle ages, from the period of Yenkei (A. D. 1308–1310) to the period of Teiwa (A. D. 1345–1349), Kao, Meicho, Josetsu, Shiubun, and others, appeared, who studied the style of the Chinese dynasties of So and Gen. This style is noted for its sketchy character; confining itself to making, by means of a few hasty strokes, a mere approximate outline of the object delineated. Afterward, and during the Ming dynasty (Chinese), the Buddhist priest Sesshu went to China and attained great fame.

Soon after this, Kano O-oinosuke Masanobu, of the province of Sagami, flourished; his son Motonobu, by his fame as an artist, rendered his family name celebrated; his descendants followed this art from age to age. The two families of Sumiyoshi and Kano continue, even at the present day, to follow this profession.

About the year A. D. 1580 a certain Iwasa Matabe, adopting the Tosa style, delineated the customs of his time; his productions are generally known as Ukiyoye (worldly pictures).

During the period of Genroku (A. D. 1688–1703), Hishigawa Moronobu, of Yedo, rendered the Matabe style popular; and Torii Kiyomitsu, Okuda Masanobu, and others, distinguished themselves in it. At the present day, the Utagawa style is very generally cultivated, although it is not much esteemed, and is also called Ukiyo.

The Medical Art (*I-gaku*).—Although in this country it is impossible to trace the healing art to its beginning, still there is no doubt but that it has existed from very ancient times; for we have Tana-muchi and Mikoto of Sukuna Hikona, both of whom were honored as deities of medicine. But no complete account of the methods they followed has descended to us; besides, owing to the fact that much has been incorrectly ascribed to them, it is very difficult to determine for what we really are indebted to them. In the reign of the Emperor Inkiyo (A. D. 412-453), Kimpa-Shinkan-Kibu, of the province of Siraki, in Corea, came over to Japan, and, possessing a knowledge of medicine, cured the emperor of his illness. After this, the Chinese medical system gradually came into use; students went abroad and acquired the arts of surgery, acupuncture, amma (i. e., dry shampooing of the body to promote a freer circulation of the blood), etc. At the same time numerous medical practitioners came over to this country, and the healing art was practised according to Chinese medical works.

The first record of the appointing of imperial court physicians is in the first year of Shucho (A. D. 686), at which time there were many who were proficient in therapeutics. After this the rules, etc., for the examination of medical students became very complete; the students being examined monthly by the professors, annually by the chief and vice-chief of the Medical Department, and again at the end of each year by the chief and vice-chief of the Imperial Household. Those who passed in all the subjects obtained the honorary rank of Ju-hachi-i-ge (a rank of the twenty-sixth degree), while those who failed in not more than two subjects obtained the honorary rank of Dai-shoi-jo (a rank of the twenty-seventh degree). The students of acupuncture ranked one degree below the medical students. Those who failed to obtain a degree at the examinations were sent back to the schools from which they had come. Similar examinations for doctors were also held in the provinces, and medical art was industriously pursued. Subsequently, however, these examinations gradually ceased. In the first year of Yenriyaku (A. D. 947) they were, by an imperial order, reëstablished, but without any great success. As time advanced, the two families of Wage and Tamba produced from age to age numerous celebrated physicians, so that at length these two families hereditarily supplied the imperial court physicians. But all their descendants did not succeed in the medical art, so that, although they successively held the posts of " medical chief" and "dispenser-in-chief," there were, nevertheless, those among them who were not qualified to fill these offices. Therefore, from time to time, outside physicians were called in to attend upon the emperor; such, for instance, as Jubutsu, Shibutsu, the Buddhist priest Kojo, and others.

In the period of Tembun (A. D. 1532-1554) there lived Manase Dosan, who was in the service of the Shogun Ashikaga Yoshiteru, and who cured the Emperor Ogi Machi of his sickness; he was called a doctor of the Tankei school.

Also at this time Osada Tokuhon became celebrated. He was a native of the province of Mikawa, was the author of the nineteen medical doctrines, and, having introduced many new ideas and making use of powerful medicines, became noted for the effectiveness of his treatment. He was the reviver of *Japanese* medical art. He died at the beginning of the period of Kuanye (A. D. 1624-1643), aged one hundred and eighteen years.

Between and during the periods of Genbun (A. D. 1736-1740) and Horeki (A. D. 1751-1763), there lived a man by the name of Hatakeyama Tamenori, of the province of Aki, who called himself Todo and changed his family name to Yoshimaru. Lamenting the decline into which the medical art had fallen, this man cleared away many long-standing errors, adopted the ancient method of the Chinese dynasty of Kan, and confined himself to the use of powerful medicines. His school was called Koho-ka (ancient method).

Before this such men as Fukui Futei, Hangino Taishiu, Mochidzuki Sanyei, Taki Angen, and others existed, who followed a method which they had formed by combining the ancient and modern systems, and which was noted for its good results.

At this time Mayeno Riyotaku, of the province of Buzen, followed the surgical profession, and, intent upon anatomy, studied with his friends Sugita Issai and Katsuragawa Hoshiu, by the aid of the interpreters at Nagasaki, some Dutch works, and, together with Udagawa Yo-an and Otsuki Gentaku, made use of Dutch medicines.

Besides introducing the use of Dutch drugs, they were the founders of the whole system of European learning existing at the present day. It is true that before them Awoki Tonsho and Arai Kimiyoshi had already made a beginning in this direction; but they did not get so far as to be able by themselves to study European books.

Materia Medica (Yakubutsu-gaku).—In the middle ages the science of drugs was not studied, as it had been in more ancient times. The first record we have concerning this science is in the "Nihonki," where it is mentioned that during the reign of the Emperor Kimmei, and about the year A. D. 540, professional searchers of medicinal herbs were sent over from Kudara, in Corea. We find that afterward there were native botanists in this country, who taught their pupils the Chinese botanical works of "Honzo," etc. Fukaye Sukeshito, Tamba Yasuyori, and others, were celebrated for their knowledge of acology. In later years, and during the period of Onin (A. D. 1467–1468), there was Takeda Sadamori, and during the period of Temmon (A. D. 1532–1554) there lived such others as Yoshida Soké, who, although they followed this art, did not render themselves conspicuous in it by the discovery or identification of medicinal plants in the Japanese flora. About the period of Genroku (A. D. 1688–1703) Kaibara Tokushin, of the province of Chikuzen, composed the botanical work "Yamato Honzo," and, shortly after, Ina Nobuoshi, of Yedo, also called Jaku Sui, composed the work "Shobutsu Ruisan," of one thousand volumes, executing himself the botanical drawings with which it is illustrated. From him Matsu-oka Gentatsu received his learning, and Matsu-oka Gentatsu was the teacher of Ono Ranzan. The shogun's government, hearing of Ranzan's fame, called him to Yedo. Many of his pupils became noted in their profession, among whom was Ito Keisuke, who continued his studies under Utagawa Yo-an, and, acquiring a knowledge of the Linnæan botanical system, introduced it into this country, where it is still in vogue. Utagawa Yo-an and Otsuki Gentaku studied European botany, and were the first to bequeath to Japan Dutch learning. Among the works of Gentaku is "Ranyen-teki-hò," in forty volumes. Among those of Yo-an is "Shokugaku-kei-gen." Besides the above-mentioned celebrities, Abe Shoo, Tamura Ransui, Hiraga Kiukei, Ota Taishiu, and others, have become renowned for their botanical studies and learning.

Surgery (Gekwa).—In ancient times surgeons were called Soshoi (doctors of wounds and sores), and this art existed as a distinct calling; but after the middle ages the distinction was abolished, and the most effectual surgical treatment was that practised by members of the two families of Wage and Tamba.

About the period of Keicho (A. D. 1596-1614), Takatori Hidetsugu flourished, and was celebrated in surgery, the followers of the system he originated being called the Takatori school. Besides this there were those who practised surgery according to the Portuguese method; these were called the Namban (foreign school). However, these systems gradually declined, and new ones were introduced by such men as Kurizaki-Shou, Narabayashi Toyoshige, etc. During and between the periods of Kiowa (A. D. 1801-1803) and Bunkua (A. D. 1804-1817), Hana-oka Dymken, of the province of Kii, invented some surgical instruments, with which he performed operations for the cure of cancer in the breast, and caries, opening the parts affected for the purpose of washing them and removing the virulent matter. By his skill he became very celebrated, and even at the present day followers of his system exist, who are called the Hana-oka school.

Doctors of Acupuncture (Harii).—At what time the art of acupuncture was first followed in this country cannot now be ascertained. But, according to the ancient imperial orders, provision is made for the appointment of a professor of acupuncture, and also for the instruction of students in this art. But few became noted for their skill in it.

In the early part of the period Yeroku (A. D. 1558-1569), Yoshida Skiu went to China to study acupuncture; and his disciples were called the Yoshida school. During the period of Bunroku (A. D. 1592-1595), Iriye Raisho studied this art under Chinese teachers, and among his pupils was Yamase Taku-ichi, who was the instructor of Sugiyama Wa-ichi.

Wa-ichi was employed by the shogun's government as a doctor of acupuncture.

Calendrography (Reki-Gaku).— The first mention of this art is in the fifteenth year of the reign of the Emperor Kimmei (A. D. 554), when, in the second month of this year, Kotoku-oson, a professor of calendrography, was sent over from Kudara in Corea.

In the tenth month of the tenth year of the reign of the Empress Suiko (A. D. 602), the Buddhist priest Kuanroku, of Kudara, brought to this country an almanac, the use of which he explained and taught to students. This almanac was called the Genka almanac. It was composed in the second year of the Chinese period of Genka (A. D. 425), of the Chinese dynasty of So, and was in use for eighty-nine years after its introduction. In the fourth year of the reign of the Empress Jito (A. D. 693), the two almanacs of "Genka" and "Giho" (i. e., "Rintoku") were in use. In the eighth month of the seventh year of Tempei-hoji (A. D. 763), and during the reign of the Emperor Junnin, the "Giho" almanac was suppressed, and in its place the Tai-yen almanac was used. This almanac was composed by the Buddhist priest Ichigiyo, during the sixteenth year of the period Kuaigen (A. D. 728) of the Chinese dynasty of To. This almanac remained in use during ninety-four years ; when, owing to inaccuracies being discovered in it, it was, upon the memorial of the calendrographer Akasuga Manomaro, suppressed in the first month of the first year of Tenan (A. D. 857), and the "Goki" almanac came into use. This was an almanac which Kaku Kenshi and others had corrected, in the first year of Ho-o (A. D. 762), of the Chinese dynasty of To. But in the sixth month of the third year of Joguan (A. D. 861), and during the reign of the Emperor Seiwa, Manamaro again memorialized the emperor, and, in consequence, the "Semmei almanac" first came into use. Later on, there were those who asserted that errors existed in this calendar ; but, owing to these errors not being minutely pointed out, and also to the fact that the office of imperial calendrographer had existed from age to age in the family of Abe, and no one else had the power of making alteration in almanacs, this almanac still continued in use.

After the lapse of eight hundred and twenty-two years, and in the first year of Teikio (A. D. 1684), there lived at Yedo Yasui Santetzu. He was noted for his skill at gô (an intricate game resembling checkers), and was also a skillful mathematician. Finding out the errors in the " Semmei " almanac, he compiled, upon the basis of the " Juji" almanac of the Chinese dynasty of Gen, the " Teikio" almanac. Afterward, and in the fourth year of Horeki (A. D. 1754), Shibakawa Dzusho re-corrected the " Teikio " almanac, and composed that of " Horeki."

Before this almanac had been long in use, the science of calendrography made rapid progress, and Takahashi Naritoki, of Yedo, and others, studying the work " Reki-sho-kosei," which had been written during the period of Koki (A. D. 1662-1722) of the Chinese dynasty of Shiu, calculated and compiled a new almanac, which they presented to the emperor in the ninth year of Kuansei (A. D. 1798). This almanac was, in the following year, distributed throughout the empire, being called the " Kuansei" almanac.

Subsequently, and in the thirteenth year of Tempo (A. D. 1842), Shibukawa Kagesuke and Adaichi Nobuaki compiled another new almanac, which was circulated in the same year, and was called the "Tempomisu-no-ye-tora " almanac.

Finally, since the sixth year of Meiji (A. D. 1873), the Gregorian calendar has come into use.

Chronometry (Rokoku-gaku).—To the ancient department of Anyorio (astronomical and calendrical department) there was attached a rokokuhakase (professor of the clepsydra), who had assistants whose duty it was to watch and keep the time.

The first clepsydra was made by the Emperor Tenji, while still a prince. In the fourth month of the tenth year of his reign (A. D. 671), this apparatus was placed on a new stand.

Such was the origin of chronometry in this country.

It is impossible to say at what date, after this, this apparatus ceased to exist, and no records remain of the manner of its construction.

It is probable that clepsydras ceased to be used after the invention of automatic-striking instruments for measuring time. On account of the invention of these more perfect instruments, clepsydras were considered as useless, and therefore no descriptions, etc., were written of them.

Automatic-striking time-keepers were first brought to China by Rieci Matteo (an Italian) during the Ming dynasty, and were first introduced into Japan during the periods of Bunroku (A. D. 1592–1595) and Keicho (1596–1614), certainly not before this time.

From the time of the clepsydra above mentioned, up to this period, it is hardly possible that no instruments existed for measuring time; still, although they may have existed, it is no doubt owing to the inconvenience of their shape, inefficient working, etc., that no minute details concerning them have descended to our days.

KAMI, OR RIYOSHI (Japanese Paper).

Although the first use of paper in this country is now unknown, still in the Japanese history, the "Nihonki," there is a record in the following words: "Paper is manufactured," referring to the eighteenth year of the reign of the Empress Suiko (A. D. 610). It is very probable that paper was first made shortly after the introduction of writing. In the "Riyo" (record of enactments) the following sentence occurs: "Six sheets of paper two feet long and one foot wide;" but it is impossible to say of what materials this paper was made.

At about the period of Yengi (A. D. 900–922) the three kinds of paper, Mashi, Hishi, and Kokushi, existed. The kind called Mashi was made from the pulp of *hempen rags*. Hishi paper was made from such plants as Gampi (*Wickstræmia canescens*), while Kokushi was made from Kodzu (*Broussonetia papyrifera*), and was similar to the paper in common use at the present time. Later on, Usugo and Atsuyo paper were manufactured; but these kinds were of the same nature as the Hishi paper. From the Kozo-plant also two kinds of papers, Danshi and Sugihara, were made; it is, however, also said that Danshi was, in ancient times, made from the Mayumi (*Euonymus Thunbergianus*).

During the middle ages Shuzenji paper, which was made at the temple of Shuzenji, in the province of Idzu, came into use.

There was also a kind of paper which was made from old paper, and was called Shukushi. In recent times many other kinds have come into use, an account and the names of which will be given in the succeeding paragraph.

PLANTS USED IN THE MANUFACTURE OF PAPER.

Kozo (*Broussonetia papyrifera.* See Fig. 1.).—The fourth order of the twenty-first class of the Linnæan system, and a genus of plants belonging to the natural order *Urticaceæ* of De Candolle. It is a small shrub, attaining about five or six feet in height, and having branches which proceed directly from the earth; it is deciduous, the new leaves appearing in spring. These leaves are of a dark-green color, ovate in form, with a sinuous or serrated margin, and very rough upon the upper surface. Of this shrub there are two kinds, pistilliferous and stameniferous. The latter kind blossom about the middle of May; this inflo-

FIG. 1.—Kozo (Broussonetia papyrifera).

FIG. 1.—Kozo (Broussonetia papyrifera).

rescence is axillary, and supported on a peduncle of a little more than an inch in length; the corolla is monopetalous, divided into four lobes at the limb, and is of a dark-purple color. These blossoms are tetrandrous.

The inflorescence of the pistilliferous plant is also supported on a peduncle, and consists of a number of flowers arranged together in a head; from each blossom a long pistil projects; their color is dark purple.

Gampi (*Wickstræmia canescens. See* Fig. 2.).—The fourth order of the eighth class of Linnæus, and a genus of plants belonging to the natural order *Thymelaceæ* of De Candolle. This plant is a deciduous shrub, which grows from about three or four feet to about ten feet in height. The leaves, which resemble the leaflets of the *Naudina domes-*

FIG. 2.—Gampi (Wickstrœmia canescens).

tica, are arranged on the stem alternately; the under surface of each is covered with soft hairs. It blossoms at about the middle of June; the inflorescence, besides being axillary, also terminates each branch, and is of a pale-yellow color. The flowers are octandrous, and have one pistil.

Mitsu Mata (Edgeworthia papyrifera. See Fig. 3.).—The first order of the eighth class of Linnæus, and a genus of the natural order *Thymelaceæ* of De Candolle. This is a deciduous shrub, which grows to about seven or eight feet in height.

Its stem and branches are trichotomous. At the close of autumn, from the ends of the branches many buds spring forth, which arrange themselves in a cluster, hanging down like a wild-bee's nest, and blos-

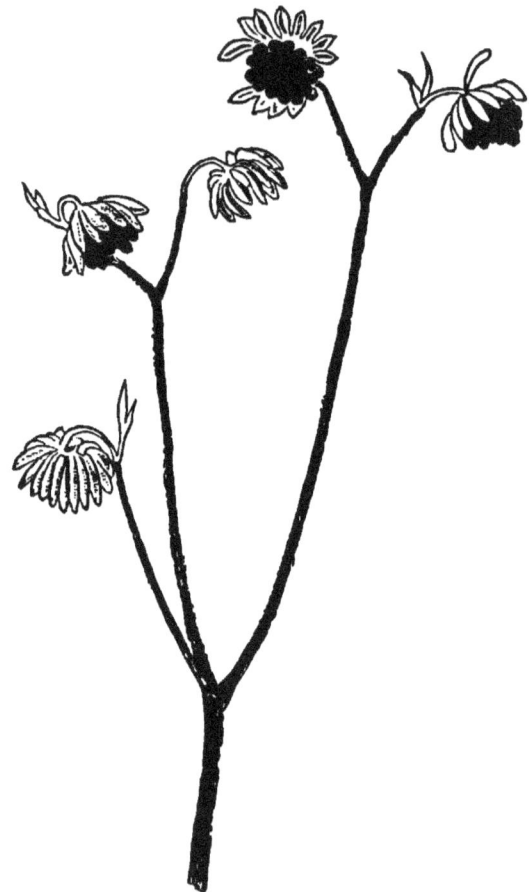

FIG. 3.—Mitsu Mata (Edgeworthia papyrifera).

som when the spring comes round. The flowers are like those of the Dzu-iko (*Daphne odora*), having four slender petals. The inside of the corolla is of a yellow color, while its outside is white.

The flower is enneandrous, and has one pistil. The leaves only appear after the blossom has fallen, and, like those of the Dzu-iko (*Daphne odora*), are large and elongated. The branches are so soft and pliant that they will not break if bent or knotted.

FIG. 4.—Tororo (Hibiscus).

Tororo (*Hibiscus. See* Fig. 4.).—The seventh order of the sixteenth class of Linnæus, a genus of *Malvaceæ* of De Candolle. This is an herbaceous plant, the seeds of which are sown in spring. It grows to the height of one or two feet, and is of a hairy nature. The leaves are palmate, having five or seven lobes, and are arranged alternately on the stem. During the hot season flowers spring from the ends and axils of the branches. The corolla has five petals, and is more than two inches in diameter; it is of a pale-yellow color, with a dark-purple blotch at the bottom of each petal, and is ephemeral. These flowers are monadelphous and polyandrous. The pod is five-celled, each cell containing many seeds. These seeds resemble those of the Ichibi (*Abutilon avicennæ*), and are of a dark-gray color. The root is conical, and abounds with viscous juice.

The Manufacture of Paper.—The plants Kozo and Gampi are cut into lengths of about three feet, are then steamed in a huge boiler, in the bottom of which there is a little boiling water. After this the bark is peeled off, and from this bark the outer pellicle is then scraped. The bark is now boiled in lye, and is then well pounded on stone blocks. After this the pulp is mixed with a certain amount of the diluted mucilage of the root of the tororo, and is placed to steep in a wooden tank. When it has remained in steep a sufficiently long time it is spread out into sheets by means of a sieve. As soon as the water has drained off from this paper, each sheet, with the aid of a straw brush, is transferred to boards to dry.

Although, according to locality and the nature of the paper manufactured, there are some differences in the details of manufacture, still the above was and is the general method employed in making it.

The following are the principal kinds:

Danshi: Of this there were two kinds, smooth and corrugated.

Hoshiyo: That made in the province of Yechizen is the best.

Sugihara: First made at Harima.

THE JAPANESE PENCIL, OR WRITING-BRUSH.

The Japanese pencil is called *fumute*, or *fude*, the latter name being most commonly used. It is also called *hananoki* (*see* Yakumo-sho), but this is only a kind of poetical name.

The origin of the Japanese pencil, or *fude*, we presume, dates from the same time as that of paper. Pencils were at first made by Chinese immigrants. In the "Record of Surnames" we find the surname of *Fude*, or pencil; those who had this surname being the descendants of Yenshokoku Yeimanko. They had the honor to receive this surname by a grant from the emperor, who was pleased with their skill.

At a later time, about the period of Taiho (A. D. 701-703), ten pencil-makers began to be employed in the "Board of Books and Writings" for manufacturing pencils there. Then, pencils were made of the hairs of rabbits, badgers, and deer. Subsequently there was a pencil-maker called Kohoshi. It is said that he made a number of large and small pencils, which he presented to the imperial court.

Manufacture.—The process of manufacturing the Japanese pencil is as follows: The hairs of certain animals being placed on the hand, are sprinkled with "pencil-powder," which consists of the ashes of burned rice-hulls, and which is exposed for sale in the same shops that deal in the hairs for pencils. Then the hairs are rubbed with both hands, cleansed from grease, equalized in length, and adjusted with a fine brass comb. After this adjustment the hairs are still further equalized with the tongue and lips, and then by means of a decoction of Funori, a kind of sea-weed used for starching, etc., made to adhere to each other, so as to form a body of about an inch and a quarter in breadth, the thickness varying according to the size of the pencils to be prepared. Then the hairs are dried, as shown in the following (Fig. 5).

Fig. 5.

If, in examining these hairs, some are found to be imperfect or in a wrong direction, these should be taken out by means of the point of a knife. The mass of the properly-adjusted hairs is then divided or separated into parcels of the size or form of a pencil. At this stage of the process, *shin*, or a paper cone, which is to keep together the hairs of the pencil, is made, and a layer of hairs (which, however, is not used in the case of inferior kinds of pencils) is laid around the paper cone, a little above its point. In the case of the Japanese pencils used during the middle ages, half their body was wound around with a piece of paper, as shown in the following (Fig. 6).

FIG. 6.

After the process of which we have given an account, the hairs are again adjusted with the mouth and collected into shape; after that, their points are rubbed repeatedly with the back of the blade of a knife, to put the hairs in order.

This process, which is called Kedsuri or Shitateru (planing or smoothing down), is the most important part in the work of pencil-making. Thus the inner layer of hairs having been adjusted, next, the exterior layer of hairs is to be laid around; a quantity of hairs which is required for that purpose being picked out by means of a knife, and combed well, is laid around the pencil, still higher up than the inner layer; the upper end of the exterior layer of hairs is then fastened with a hemp-thread, one end of which is inserted in the pencil stem or holder with the upper ends of the now brush-shaped hairs, and the pencil is ready for use.

INKSTONE.

The inkstone, called in Japanese Sumisuri, Suzuri, or Miru-ishi, was invented about the same time as the pencil. At first, however, ink-stones were mostly made of earthen-ware, good inkstones, properly so called, being of later origin. Thus, for instance, those in use at the Daijokuan, as well as even those brought to the imperial palace, were all of earthen-ware. Afterward, it appears, a little before the periods of Genko (A. D. 1321–1323) and Kemmu (A. D. 1334–1335), the true inkstone was coming into general use; and it is at about the same period that we first find Saga-ishi, Shiaku-o-ji-ishi, and Tosa-ishi (stones very valuable for the inkstones), held in great estimation.

Besides the above stones, we have many other kinds of which the inkstone can be made, and of which we shall presently give the names.

Manufacture.—In the first process a stone is cut into even slabs by two persons, who sit opposite to each other, with an instrument. Then the stone thus cut up is polished with a white whetstone, on which a quantity of sea-sand is spread out. The "ink-pond," or the part of the inkstone in which the ink is kept, is cut with a large chisel, to which the workman applies his shoulder in working it. When this process is nearly finished, and the "ink-pond" is formed, it is again pared with the hand-chisel, and then polished with a blue whetstone. In the case of superior kinds of inkstones, the inside and outside of the "ink-pond," as well as other parts, are polished with a whetstone called Nagura, and with a small stone, with which the workman finishes off the hollow parts.

MATERIALS FOR INKSTONE.

Tosa: It is a kind of marine stone, usually containing something like copper and iron, the absence of which, however, is a requisite for stones of best quality.

Shiaku-o-ji: It is found in the province of Tamba; it has silvery veins running through it lengthwise. The ready darkening of the veins is a mark of the inferior quality of the stone. This inferior quality is produced from some newly-discovered quarries, and cannot be compared with that which comes from the old and celebrated quarries of Tamba.

Amebata: This stone comes from the province of Kai; there are two sorts of it, respectively called Okuyama and Hashiyama, the former being the better of the two.

Hosoku: This stone comes from the province of Wakasa; the best kinds are hard to be obtained. It is sometimes called Takata-ishi, and is of a red color.

Tsukinowa: This stone comes from the province of Yamashiro.

Takao: This stone comes from the same province.

Takashima: This stone comes from the province of Omi.

Nikko-ishi: This stone comes from the Nikko Mountain; it is of a jet-black color, and the best material, but rather hard.

Sakurakawa: This stone comes from Numata, the province of Kodzuke.

Kansui: This stone comes from the province of Hitachi. There is another kind resembling this, called *Shima Kansui.*

Kuroyama: This stone comes from the province of Mutsu; the hard and fine quality is difficult to be obtained.

Kinho-ishi: This stone comes from the province of Mikawa.

Yoro: This comes from the province of Mino.

Uchiyama-ishi: This comes from the province of Bungo; the best sorts of it are exceedingly rare.

Takata: This comes from the province of Mimasaku; there are some very old inkstones made of the best kinds of this stone.

Kamokawa-ishi: This comes from the province of Yamashiro.

Takanokawa-ishi: This comes from the same province.

Kagami-ishi: This comes from the province of Ise; it is vulgarly called *Sasameno.*

Futami-ishi: This comes from the province of Ise; it is something like *Shirahama* (a kind of stone), but softer.

Shira-ishi: This comes from the province of Higo.

Shirahama-ishi: This comes from the province of Kii.

Takahama: This comes from the province of Hizen.

Konoha-ishi: This comes from the province of Yechigo, and several other places.

Takayama-ishi: This comes from the province of Bingo.

Akama: This comes from the province of Nagato.

Manjiu-ishi: This comes from Iwaki.

Shohoji-ishi: This comes from the province of Rikuchiu; it is of a rather rough nature, but well suited to rub the ink on.

Okatsu: This comes from the province of Ugo; it is black.

Nobe-oka-ishi: This comes from the province of Hiyuga.

Tamba Kuro-ishi: This comes from the province of Tamba; it is somewhat like Amabata stone. It is brought from some newly-discovered quarries.

Nagarekawa-ishi: This comes from the province of Kai; it is a sort of Amabata stone, being of a purple color.

Fukazawa-ishi: This comes from the province of Shinano; it is of the same kind as the Amabata stone.

Tsukubaishi: This comes from the province of Hitachi; it is like Takashima-ishi.

Bushu Kuro-ishi: This comes from the province of Musashi.

Ishimaki-ishi: This comes from the province of Mutsu; it is of a black color.

Kinsei-ishi: This comes from the province of Kodzuke; it is like the stone of the same name found in Liyobisan, China.

Kawagoi-ishi: This comes from the province of Musashi; it is of a gray color, and of the same nature as that produced from the province of Omi.

JAPANESE INK.

The origin of the Japanese ink dates from the same period as that of paper and the pencil, the processes of making them all having been introduced into this country from China.

During the middle ages the ink used in public or government offices was manufactured in the "Board of Books and Writings," and the process of making it was the same as that which we use at the present day. At later periods, Musa ink, made in the province of Omi, Kaibara ink, made in the province of Tamba, as well as Taihei ink, made in the province of Yamashiro, were very noted for their superiority to others. Again, at a still later time, lamp-black ink (i. e., ink made of lamp-black) was invented in Nara, the southern capital, and has ever since been a celebrated article of production of that place.

Manufacture of Ink.—The material for the ink, whether it be lamp-black or so-called pine-smoke, i. e., soot obtained by the imperfect combustion of pine-wood, is worked into a proper consistency by combining it with glue and water. At first, the lamp-black or pine-smoke which is thus worked with glue and water does not readily come into a mass, still being in a dry state and separated and scattered—a state which indicates the proper proportions of the mixture of those ingredients. After being kneaded repeatedly, however, it comes into a mass somewhat like dough. This process is performed on a plank, which in winter should have a fire below it, in order to prevent the congelation of the glue. When the material has been worked into a perfect consistency, it is put into the ink-mould, which is made of wood, and consists of two parts, one being called the higher and the other the lower, and is pressed by a heavy stone bearing on it, or by a press. It depends on the thoroughness of this process whether the figures on the surfaces of the cakes of ink stand out clearly or not. After this the cakes of ink are taken from the mould and put in a mass of very slightly-moistened ashes. After having been kept in the moist ashes for four hours, the cakes are transferred to a mass of dry ashes for one day; after this, the ink is put into a mass of perfectly dry ashes for three days, at the expiration of which it is taken out and washed clean with cold water. After having been dried and polished, the whole process is finished, and the ink ready to be used.

To obtain lamp-black, lamps are placed in regular order on a shelf, and are covered with unglazed porcelain receivers. The lamp-black which thus collects upon the receivers is regularly scraped off from time to time; if too much time were allowed to pass before scraping it off, the lamp-black would become a solid mass, and be useless.

As to the kind of oil used for obtaining lamp-black, that of the *Sesamum orientalis* is the best, that of the rape-seed being next.

The collecting of the soot of pine-wood used in manufacturing ink is performed as follows: A plastered house of three or four *ken* (one *ken* being seventy-one and a half inches English) is built, in which partitions are made, and the four walls of which are pasted over with some kind of coarse paper. The ground is paved with stone, on which the resinous boughs of the pine are burned after having been split into slender pieces. The soot which collects on the paper is scraped off in due time.

The Engraving of Books.—The first engraving of books took place in the third month of the first year of Hoki (A. D. 770), when "Darani" (a Buddhist book written in Pali characters), of the Hiakuman Towers, was engraved; but since then we do not hear of any book being engraved till the third day of the sixth month in the first year of Kuangen (A. D. 1243), when the engraved "Hokekiyo" (a Buddhist book) was offered to the Buddhist gods; next to it, "Sentakushu" (the Buddhist book of the Jodo sect) and the "Confucian Analects" were engraved one after the other. It was not till the eighth year of Genroku (A. D. 1695) that any book was printed with five kinds of colors.

APPENDIX.

I. CONSTITUTION OF THE MOMBUSHO, OR JAPANESE DEPARTMENT OF EDUCATION.

THE Mombusho is a department of the Government for the administration of the educational affairs of the empire. Its duties are:

1. To manage government schools and colleges.
2. To supervise public and private local schools.
3. To collect and diffuse educational information.

The organization of the department is as follows:

Kio (Minister of Education), whose duties are:

1. To superintend the officials and the business of the department, and to administer the educational affairs of the empire.
2. To propose to the Government measures in regard to education; to nominate for appointment, promotion, and dismissal, all officials above and including the seventh rank; and to appoint or dismiss, of his own motion, all officials below the seventh rank.

Tayu (Senior Vice-Minister of Education, and
Shoyu (Junior Vice-Minister of Education):

Whose duties are to assist the Minister of Education in discharging his duties, and, when required, to perform the duties of minister.

Daijo (First Secretary),
Gon-daijo (Second Secretary),
Shojo (First Junior Secretary), and
Gon-shojo (Second Junior Secretary):

Whose duties are to conduct the business of the department under the direction of the minister, and to preserve and keep in order all public documents.

Dairoku (Chief Clerk).
Gon-dairoku (Second Chief Clerk).
Chiuroku (Middle Clerk).
Gon-chiuroku (Second Middle Clerk).
Shoroku (Junior Clerk).
Gon-shoroku (Second Junior Clerk).
Hissei (Scribe).
Seisho (Miscellaneous Business).

Connected with the department of Education is the Bureau of Superintendence, called the Tokugakuyoku, containing the following officers:

Dai-Tokugaku (Chief Superintendent),
Chiu-Tokugaku (Second Superintendent), and
Sho-Tokugaku (Third Superintendent):

    Whose duties are to superintend educational matters, and to inspect and cause to be inspected the schools under the department.

Dai-Shigaku (Chief Inspector),
Chiu-Shigaku (Second Inspector), and
Sho-Shigaku (Third Inspector):

    Whose duties are to inspect and supervise the educational business of the several school-districts.

Dai-Shoki (Chief Clerk),
Chiu-Shoki (Second Clerk), and
Sho-Shoki (Third Clerk):

    Whose duties are to transact the business of the office, and to preserve and keep in order the public records.

REGULATIONS FOR THE TRANSACTION OF BUSINESS.

The business of the department is divided into two classes. The business of the first class is transacted by the minister after the approval of the General Government. The business of the second class is conducted at the discretion of the minister, who is, however, responsible for all the business both of the first and second classes.

Business of the First Class.—To devise and establish systems of education; to make and revise educational regulations; to establish school taxation; to regulate the grants of money to local school-districts; to establish

APPENDIX. 179

government schools; to send officials of the department to foreign countries, etc.

Business of the Second Class.—To present educational measures to the General Government; to issue notifications concerning the business of the department; to supervise the local authorities in regard to educational matters; to confer academic degrees; to regulate the disbursement of government grants to the school-districts; to collect books and apparatus conducive to the progress of science and the arts; to collect and diffuse information in regard to education; to summon conventions of inspectors of school-directors, or of school-teachers and school-experts, for the purposes of discussion of educational questions; to send students to foreign countries and to superintend the same; to engage native and foreign teachers, and to regulate their salaries, etc.

II. CHRONICLE OF EVENTS IN THE RECENT HISTORY OF THE DEPARTMENT OF EDUCATION.

AT the time of the restoration of the Government, the subject of education was intrusted to an Educational Board, which administered the affairs connected with this branch of the Government from the first to the fourth year of Meiji (A. D. 1868-1871). On account of the disturbances caused by the civil war which existed in the country in 1868, educational matters were in a very unsettled condition. Many of the school-buildings had been occupied for army-quarters, and the medical schools and hospitals were occupied with the care of the sick and wounded.

In November, 1868, the Foreign-Language School, which had been established by the shogun's government, in Yedo, was reopened under the new Educational Board. Foreign languages were taught in part by native and in part by foreign teachers.

In December, 1868, the old College of Confucius, founded by the shogun's government, was also reopened, under the name of Shoheiko. It was about this time that Yamanouchi Yodo, the Daimio of Toza, was appointed chief of the Educational Board, and the offices of secretary and second secretary, as well as professors of the first, second, and third ranks, were created. From this time the Foreign-Language School and the Medical School and hospital came under the control of the Educational Board.

In February, 1869, the publication of newspapers was placed under the charge of the Educational Board, and rules therefor were issued, and in May following the publication of books was in like manner intrusted to it.

In June, 1869, it was ordered by the Government that the Shoheiko (College of Confucius) was to be hereafter called Daigakko (the university), and should take the place of the ancient national university as the head of the educational system. The offices of the temporary Educational Board were thereupon abolished, and corresponding ones connected with the university were created.

In July, 1869, several of the professors in the Confucian college and the Foreign-Language School were selected as members of the Assembly composed of representatives from the provincial governments.

In October, 1869, a Bureau of Translation was created in the Foreign-Language School, for the purpose of translating and compiling text-books from foreign languages.

In December, 1869, the Foreign-Language School and Medical School were ordered to be called respectively the South College and North College. At the same time several new offices, both of administration and instruction, were created, the chief of them being Daigaku-no-Betsto, which position was held by Matsudaira Shungaku, Prince of Yechizen.

In February, 1870, school-laws in relation to colleges, high-schools, and primary schools, were proclaimed. This was the first attempt, after the restoration of the Government, to make general laws in regard to the education of the country. This was an evidence of the interest manifested in the education of the people by the emperor and his government.

In July, 1870, it was ordered that each of the provincial governments should select one or more pupils who were promising scholars, to be sent to the Foreign-Language School to be educated at the government expense.

In August, 1870, several of the most advanced students in the English and French sections of the Foreign-Language School were sent abroad to be educated in Western science and literature at the government expense; and in November of the same year a few students were sent from the Medical College for the purpose of studying medicine in Europe. In December it was further ordered that all the students studying abroad, whether sent by the central or local governments, should be under the control of the Educational Board.

In January, 1871, the work of compiling a complete English-and-Japanese dictionary was begun under the Educational Board.

In June, 1871, orders were given to the Medical College to send medical officers into the several parts of the country, for the purpose of taking control for the college of all matters connected with medicine.

During this same month the most important step was taken in the progress of education. It was deemed by the Government that the education of the people was of sufficient importance to be intrusted to a distinct department of the Government; hence, in the place of the old Educational Board, a Department of Education (Mombusho) was organized. All powers relating to educational affairs were vested in this department. Elementary and higher instruction, the management of schools and colleges, were intrusted to its charge. Yeto Shimpei was created Vice-Minister of Education, and most of the old officers, both in the Foreign-Language and Medical Schools, were continued in their positions under the Department of Education. The old quarters of the Educational Board were used by the new department. The authority of the department was extended over the schools of Osaka and at Nagasaki, as well as over the students studying abroad. Matters connected with medical education and the public health were in like manner put under its control.

In this same month (June, 1871) Oki Takato was appointed Minister of Education. The students who had been sent abroad by the several provincial governments were now, on account of the change of these governments, left to the control of the Department of Education; and, as they were more numerous than the department could properly support, it was determined to recall them and send them out under new regulations.

In August, 1871, the elementary and high schools in Tokio were placed under the direct charge of the Department of Education. This, however, was only temporary, as, after the issue of the code of education in 1872, they were restored to the control of the Tokio local government.

It was in this month that Yeto Shimpei, who had been Vice-Minister of Education, was relieved from duty, and appointed a senator of the first rank.

In September, 1871, a Bureau for the Compilation of Text-Books was created in the Department of Education. New regulations were at this time made for the Foreign-Language and Medical Schools. The mixed system of Japanese and European instruction was modified, so that all the scholars were taught according to the foreign method and by competent teachers. It was also determined that the method of appointing students by the provincial governments be abolished, and that hereafter all persons might be admitted to the schools on passing a satisfactory examination. It was, moreover, determined, in order to encourage scholarship, that promising students who obtained a high standing should be sent abroad to complete their courses of study.

In October, 1871, a Bureau of Vaccination was established in the Tokio Medical School.

In November, 1871, Tanaka Fujimaro, then chief secretary of the Department of Education, was sent to America and Europe in connection with the embassy, as a commissioner to investigate and report upon educational matters in foreign countries. A report was made on his return, giving in detail his observations, which has been printed and published.

In February, 1872, a building for a female school in Tokio was completed and opened under the charge of the Department of Education. Up to this time the education of women had not received the same government support as that of men, and therefore this first step in providing better facilities was an important event in the history of education. This school was designed to provide education both in Japanese and English.

In April, 1872, a library was opened at the seat of the College of Confucius, and the public admitted free.

In May of the same year the Tokio Normal School was established and opened. It was designed to train teachers for the elementary schools, which, under the new orders of the department, were to be taught in accordance with more approved methods. The students admitted to the Normal School were supported at the expense of the Government.

In August, 1872, the new educational laws were proclaimed throughout Japan. These laws are still in force. The old schools maintained under the direction of the local governments were by these laws to be replaced by others modeled after the regulations of the department, and pursuing definite courses of instruction.

The sum of two million yens was appropriated by the General Government for the expenses of the Department of Education, and for the educational institutions under its charge.

In October, 1872, a Bureau of Superintendence was organized in Tokio, to inspect and supervise the schools.

Oki Takato was appointed Minister of Religion in addition to the office of Minister of Education, and the offices of the Department of Education were removed to the same building as was occupied by that of the Department of Religion.

In November, 1872, an educational convention was held in the buildings of the department, composed of the educational officers of the local governments. They discussed the school-laws and their practical working. A result of this convention was the determination by the department, in order to give the people greater facilities for education, hereafter to appropriate certain sums of money to the local governments, in proportion to the population, to be used for the support of elementary schools. The quota fixed at that time was nine-tenths of a cent per capita.

In February, 1873, the department issued orders to the local governments in regard to the divisions of the grand-school districts into middle and elementary school districts, and also in regard to the number of elementary schools already established, and the regulations and mode of maintenance of the same.

The Government made its semi-annual appropriation to the Department of Education for school purposes, being at the reduced rate of one million three hundred thousand yens per year.

The chief secretary, Tanaka Fujimaro, sent out as commissioner of education, returned to Japan, and was soon after appointed to the office of Shoyu, or junior vice-minister.

The publication of the gazette of the department was begun. It was designed to contain accounts of the systems and progress of education, and such information in regard to foreign and native education as might be of value.

In April, 1873, the following alterations were announced in regard to the divisions of the grand-school districts, and the principal educational seats in them : The grand-school districts were reduced from eight to seven, and the boundaries readjusted. In the first grand-school district, Tokio was made the principal seat of learning ; in the second, Aichi ; in the third, Osaka ; in the fourth, Hiroshima ; in the fifth, Nagasaki ; in the sixth, Niigata ; and in the seventh, Miyagi.

Oki Takato, the Minister of Education, was made one of the Cabinet Council, and therefore ceased to be minister, whereupon the junior vice-minister Tanaka became acting chief.

The Tokio Foreign-Language School was separated into two parts; the first to be called the Tokio Kaisei Gakko, and to be organized as a university, where general science and literature, as well as special courses in law, chemical technology, engineering, polytechnic science, and mining, were to be pursued; the second part to continue as a school of foreign languages, and to provide instruction in the English, French, German, Russian, and Chinese languages.

In May and June, 1873, educational officers were sent from the department to visit and inspect the schools in the first, third, fourth, fifth, sixth, and seventh grand-school districts.

In July, 1873, the Tokugakuyoku, or Bureau of Superintendence, was established in the Department of Education, the business of which was the inspection of the schools under the department.

In August, 1873, two additional normal schools were founded, one at Osaka, and one at Miyagi, the latter of which, however, was not opened until some time later.

For the purpose of making better regulations in regard to physicians in the country, orders were issued that each local government should report to the Department of Education the names and number of physicians, and also other information concerning medical matters within its jurisdiction. A medical laboratory was also established in the Tokio Medical College.

Dr. David Murray, of the United States, having arrived in Japan, entered upon his duties as superintendent of educational affairs.

Among other amendments in regard to the grade of officers and instructors the following academic ranks were established, viz.: *Hakase* (Doctor), *Gakushi* (Master), and *Tokugeyioshi* (Bachelor), to be conferred by the Department of Education.

In the same month the new buildings were completed for the Kaisei Gakko (University of Tokio), and were opened with appropriate ceremonies by his majesty the emperor, accompanied by high officers of the Government.

During this month her majesty the empress visited the University of Tokio and the Tokio Female School, and witnessed the exercises of the students.

It was determined from this time that the students who had been sent abroad at the expense of the Government should be recalled, with a view to send others better qualified, and selected from those who had been educated in the home institutions. Orders were therefore sent for their recall at the earliest time.

In January, 1874, Kido Takiyoshi was appointed Minister of Education in addition to his office of cabinet councilor.

In February of this year a department of industrial arts was established in the University of Tokio. It was to be conducted in the Japanese language, and to give instruction in the chemical and mechanical arts.

Four additional normal schools were founded by the Department of Education, viz., at Aichi, Hiroshima, Nagasaki, and Niigata; and in the month following foreign-language schools were established in Aichi, Hiroshima, Niigata, and Miyagi; thus in each of the seven grand-school districts there were now a normal school and a foreign-language school.

In March, 1874, the Tokio Female Normal School was established by the Department of Education. Her majesty the empress had indicated her wish to contribute the sum of five thousand yens from her private purse for the purpose of promoting the education of her sex in the empire. She therefore gave this amount to the department toward the establishment of the Female Normal School. Accordingly, buildings were erected, and in October of the following year were dedicated by the empress in person.

A Bureau for the Examination of Medicines was established in the city of Tokio under the Department of Education.

In May, 1874, Kido Takiyoshi resigned the office of Minister of Education.

In September Tanaka Fujimaro was advanced to the rank of Tayu, or Senior Vice-Minister of Education.

The arrangement of bureaus in the department was modified as follows: 1. Bureau of Schools. 2. Bureau of Finance. 3. Bureau of Publication. 4. Bureau of Copyright and Press Laws. 5. Bureau of Public Health.

The Medical School and Hospital at Nagasaki, which had been under the control of the Department of Education, was transferred to the local government.

In December, 1874, all the foreign-language schools except that at Tokio were constituted English-language schools. That at Tokio was divided into two schools, the one an English-language school, the other a foreign-language school for instruction in French, German, Russian, and Chinese.

In January, 1875, the amount appropriated by the Government to the Department of Education was fixed at two million yens per year, and the sum contributed by the department to the local governments for the support of elementary eduction was fixed at seventy thousand yens.

A Bureau for the Examination of Medicine was in February established at Kioto, and in March at Osaka.

The museum, library, and botanical garden, which had hitherto been under the joint control of the Department of Education and the Department of Home Affairs, were transferred to the superintendence of the former ; and in June the Bureaus of Public Health and of Copyright and Press Laws were transferred to the Department of Home Affairs.

In July, 1875, three officers were sent out to America to investigate the methods of conducting normal schools. From the highest class also in the University of Tokio, students were sent out to continue their education in special branches, viz., nine in America, one in France, and one in Germany.

The semi-annual appropriation from the General Government to the Department of Education was made on the scale of one million seven hundred thousand yens per annum.

In November of this year the constitution and limitations of the authority of the Department of Education were revised and proclaimed by the General Government.

III. LIST OF EMPERORS.

NAME.	Date from Jimmu.	Date, Christian Era.	NAME.	Date from Jimmu.	Date, Christian Era.
Jimmu...............	1	B.C. 660	Seiwa...............	1519	859
Suisei...............	79	581	Yozei...............	1537	877
Annei...............	112	548	Kuoko..............	1545	885
Itoku...............	150	510	Uta................	1553	888
Koshio..............	185	475	Daigo...............	1558	898
Ko-an...............	268	392	Sujaku..............	1591	931
Korei...............	370	290	Muragami...........	1607	947
Kogen...............	446	214	Rezei...............	1628	968
Kaikua..............	503	157	Yenyu...............	1630	970
Sujin...............	563	97	Kuazan..............	1645	985
Suinin...............	629	A.D. 29	Ichijo...............	1647	987
Keiko...............	731	71	Sanjo...............	1672	1012
Seimu...............	791	131	Go Ichi-jo...........	1677	1017
Chu-ai..............	852	192	Go Suzaku...........	1697	1037
Jingo (empress)......	861	201	Go Rezei............	1706	1046
Ojin.................	930	270	Go Sanjo............	1729	1069
Nintoku.............	973	313	Shirakawa...........	1733	1073
Richu...............	1060	400	Horikawa............	1747	1087
Hansei...............	1065	405	Toba................	1769	1108
Inkiyo...............	1071	411	Shutoku.............	1784	1124
Anko................	1113	453	Konoye..............	1802	1142
Yariyaku............	1116	456	Go Shirakawa........	1816	1156
Seinei...............	1140	480	Nijo.................	1819	1159
Kenso...............	1145	485	Rokujo..............	1826	1166
Ninken...............	1148	488	Takakura............	1829	1169
Buretsu..............	1159	499	Antoku..............	1841	1181
Keitai...............	1167	507	Gotoba..............	1846	1186
Ankan...............	1194	534	Tsuchi-mikado.......	1859	1199
Senka...............	1196	536	Juntoku.............	1871	1211
Kimmei..............	1200	540	Chukiyo.............	1882	1222
Bitatsu..............	1232	572	Yojo.................	1893	1233
Yomei...............	1246	586	Go Saga.............	1903	1243
Shujun...............	1248	588	Go Fukakusa.........	1907	1247
Suiko (empress)......	1253	593	Kameyama...........	1926	1260
Jomei...............	1289	629	Go-uta..............	1936	1276
Kokiyoku............	1302	642	Fushimi..............	1948	1288
Kotoku...............	1305	645	Go Fushimi..........	1959	1299
Saimio...............	1315	655	Go Nijo..............	1961	1301
Tenji.................	1328	668	Hanazono............	1968	1308
Kobun...............	1332	672	Go Daigo............	1979	1319
Tenmu...............	1333	673			
Jito (empress)........	1350	690	SOUTHERN DYNASTY.[1]		
Monmu...............	1357	697	Go Komuragami......	1999	1339
Genmei (empress)....	1368	708	Go Kameyama.......	2028	1368
Gensho "	1375	715			
Jomu................	1384	724	NORTHERN DYNASTY.		
Koken (empress).....	1409	749	Komio...............	1996	1336
Junnin...............	1419	759	Shuko...............	2009	1349
Koken (reënthroned).	1425	765	Go Kogen............	2012	1352
Konin................	1430	770	Go Yenyu............	2032	1372
Kuanmu..............	1442	782	Go Komats...........	2043	1383
Heijo.................	1466	806			
Saga.................	1470	810	Go Komats...........	2053	1393
Ninna................	1484	824	Shioko...............	2073	1413
Ninmio...............	1494	834	Go Hanazono........	2089	1429
Montoku.............	1511	851	Go Tsuchi-mikado....	2125	1465

[1] There were two dynasties during the period (1336-1392 A.D.), which were reunited in the Emperor Go Komats.

APPENDIX.

LIST OF EMPERORS.—(Continued.)

NAME.	Date from Jimmu.	Date, Christian Era.	NAME.	Date from Jimmu.	Date, Christian Era.
Go Kashiwabara	2161	1501	Naka-mikado	2370	1710
Go Nara	2187	1527	Sakuramachi	2396	1736
Omasaki	2218	1558	Momosono	2407	1747
Go Yozei	2247	1587	Go Sakuramachi (empress)	2423	1763
Go Midzunowo	2272	1612	Go Momosono	2431	1771
Miojo (empress)	2290	1630	Kokuaku	2440	1780
Go Komio	2304	1644	Ninko	2477	1817
Gozai-in	2315	1655	Komio	2507	1847
Reigen	2323	1663	Mutsuhito	2527	1867
Tozan	2347	1687	Present year	2536	1876

IV. LIST OF YEAR-PERIODS.

NAME.	Date of Beginning from the Emperor Jimmu.	Date of Beginning from Christian Era.	NAME.	Date of Beginning from the Emperor Jimmu.	Date of Beginning from Christian Era.
Taikua	1305	A.D. 645	Yencho	1583	923
Hakuchi	1310	650	Shiohei	1591	931
Sujaka	1332	672	Tengio	1598	938
Hakuho	1333	673	Ten Riyaku	1607	947
Shucho	1346	686	Tentoku	1617	957
Taikua	1355	695	Wowa	1621	961
Taicho	1357	697	Koho	1624	964
Taiho	1361	701	Anwa	1628	968
Kei-un	1364	704	Tenroku	1630	970
Wado	1368	708	Tenyen	1633	973
Hoki	1375	715	Jogen	1636	976
Yozo	1377	717	Tengen	1638	978
Jinki	1384	724	Yeikuan	1643	983
Tenpio	1389	729	Kuanwa	1645	985
Tenpio Shoho	1409	749	Yeiyen	1647	987
Tenpio Hoji	1417	757	Yeiso	1649	989
Tenpio Jingo	1425	765	Shioriyaku	1650	990
Jingo Kei-un	1427	767	Chotoku	1655	995
Hoki	1430	770	Choho	1659	999
Teno	1441	781	Kuanko	1664	1004
Yenriyaku	1442	782	Chowa	1672	1012
Daido	1466	806	Kuannin	1677	1017
Kuonin	1470	810	Chian	1681	1021
Tencho	1484	824	Manju	1684	1024
Jowa	1494	834	Chogen	1688	1028
Kasho	1508	848	Choriyaku	1697	1037
Nin-ju	1511	851	Chokiu	1700	1040
Saiko	1514	854	Kuantoku	1704	1044
Tenan	1517	857	Yenjo	1706	1046
Jokuan	1519	859	Tenki	1713	1053
——	1537	877	Kohei	1718	1058
Ninna	1545	885	Chiriyaku	1725	1065
Kuanpei	1549	889	Yenkiu	1729	1069
Shiotai	1558	898	Joho	1734	1074
Yengi	1561	901	Joriyaku	1737	1077

APPENDIX.

LIST OF YEAR-PERIODS.—(Continued.)

NAME.	Date of Beginning from the Emperor Jimmu.	Date of Beginning from Christian Era.	NAME.	Date of Beginning from the Emperor Jimmu.	Date of Beginning from Christian Era.
Yeiho	1741	1081	Kuanki	1889	1229
Otoku	1744	1084	Joyei	1892	1232
Kuanji	1747	1087	Tenpuku	1893	1233
Kaho	1754	1094	Bunriyaku	1894	1234
Yeicho	1756	1096	Katei	1895	1235
Shotoku	1757	1097	Riyakunin	1898	1238
Kowa	1759	1099	Yenwo	1899	1239
Choji	1764	1104	Ninji	1900	1240
Kajo	1766	1106	Kuangen	1903	1243
Tennin	1768	1108	Hoji	1907	1247
Tenyei	1770	1110	Kencho	1909	1249
Yeikiu	1773	1113	Kogen	1916	1256
Genyei	1778	1118	Shoka	1917	1257
Ho-an	1780	1120	Shogen	1919	1259
Tenji	1784	1124	Bunwo	1920	1260
Daiji	1786	1126	Kocho	1921	1261
Tensho	1791	1131	Bunyei	1924	1264
Chosho	1792	1132	Kenji	1935	1275
Hoyen	1795	1135	Ko-an	1938	1278
Yeiji	1801	1141	Showo	1948	1288
Koji	1802	1142	Yeinin	1953	1293
Tenyo	1804	1144	Sho-an	1959	1299
Kiuan	1805	1145	Kengen	1962	1302
Ninpei	1811	1151	Kagen	1963	1303
Kinju	1814	1154	Tokuji	1966	1306
Hogen	1816	1156	Yenkei	1968	1308
Heiji	1819	1159	Ocho	1971	1311
Yeiriyaku	1820	1160	Showa	1972	1312
Oyei	1821	1161	Bunpo	1977	1317
Chokuan	1823	1163	Genwo	1979	1319
Yeiman	1825	1165	Genko	1981	1321
Ninan	1826	1166	Shochu	1984	1324
Kawo	1829	1169	Kareki	1986	1326
Sho-an	1831	1171	Gentoku	1989	1329
Angen	1835	1175	Genko	1991	1331
Jijo	1837	1177	Kenmu	1994	1334
Yowa	1841	1181	SOUTHERN DYNASTY.[1]		
Juyei	1842	1182			
Monji	1845	1185	Yengen	1996	1336
Kenkiu	1856	1190	Kokoku	2000	1340
Shoji	1859	1199	Shohei	2006	1346
Kennin	1861	1201	Kentoku	2030	1370
Genkin	1864	1204	Bunchu	2032	1372
Kenyei	1866	1206	Tenju	2035	1375
Shogen	1867	1207	Kowa	2041	1381
Kenriyaku	1871	1211	Genchu	2044	1384
Kenpo	1873	1213			
Jokiu	1879	1219	NORTHERN DYNASTY.		
Jowo	1882	1222	Rekiwo	1998	1338
Gennin	1884	1224	Koyei	2002	1342
Karoku	1885	1225	Teiwa	2005	1345
Antei	1887	1227	Kuanwo	2010	1350

[1] There were two dynasties during the time (1336–1399 A. D.), and separate year-periods were used.

APPENDIX.

LIST OF YEAR-PERIODS.—(Continued.)

NAME.	Date of Beginning from the Emperor Jimmu.	Date of Beginning from Christian Era.	NAME.	Date of Beginning from the Emperor Jimmu.	Date of Beginning from Christian Era.
Yenbun	2016	1356	Genna	2275	1615
Owa	2021	1361	Kuanyei	2284	1624
Toji	2022	1362	Shoho	2304	1644
O-an	2028	1368	Kei-an	2308	1648
Yeiwa	2035	1375	Showo	2312	1652
Koreki	2039	1379	Meireki	2315	1655
Yeitoku	2041	1381	Manji	2318	1658
Shitoku	2044	1384	Kuanbun	2321	1661
Kakei	2047	1387	Yenpo	2333	1673
Kowo	2049	1389	Tenwa	2341	1681
Miotoku	2050	1390	Jokio	2344	1684
Oyen	2054	1394	Tenroku	2348	1688
Seicho	2088	1428	Hoyei	2364	1704
Yeikiyo	2089	1429	Shotoku	2371	1711
Kakitsu	2101	1441	Hokio	2376	1716
Bunan	2104	1444	Genbun	2396	1736
Hotoku	2109	1449	Kuanpo	2401	1741
Kiotoku	2112	1452	Yenkio	2404	1744
Kosho	2115	1455	Kuanyen	2408	1748
Choroku	2117	1457	Horeki	2411	1751
Kuansho	2120	1460	Meiwa	2424	1764
Bunsho	2126	1466	Anyei	2432	1772
Onin	2127	1467	Tenmei	2441	1781
Bunmei	2129	1469	Kuansei	2449	1789
Chokio	2147	1487	Kiowa	2461	1801
Yentoku	2149	1489	Bunkua	2464	1804
Miowo	2152	1492	Bunsei	2478	1818
Bunki	2161	1501	Tenpo	2490	1830
Yeisei	2164	1504	Koka	2504	1844
Taiyei	2181	1521	Kayei	2508	1848
Kioroku	2188	1528	Ansei	2514	1854
Tenbun	2192	1532	Manyei	2520	1860
Koji	2215	1555	Bunkiu	2521	1861
Yeiroku	2218	1558	Genji	2524	1864
Genki	2230	1570	Keiwo	2525	1865
Tensho	2233	1573	Meiji	2528	1868
Bunroku	2252	1592	Meiji, ninth year	2536	1876
Keicho	2256	1596			

APPENDIX. 191

V. CATALOGUE OF ARTICLES EXHIBITED BY THE JAPANESE DEPARTMENT OF EDUCATION AT THE INTERNATIONAL EXHIBITION, 1876.

1. EDUCATIONAL HISTORY.

1. Manuscript Outline History of Japanese Education. English translation.

2. Manuscript History of Japanese Literature, Science, and Arts. Abridged English translation.

3. Chronicle of Events in the History of the Department of Education. English translation.

2. EDUCATIONAL LAWS AND NOTIFICATIONS.

1. Code of Education. Issued in 1872.

2. Collection of Educational Notifications, 1871-1875.

3. Notifications to local authorities and to government schools, 1873-1875.

4. Constitution of the Department of Education, and regulations for the transaction of business. English translation.

3. EDUCATIONAL REPORTS.

1. First Annual Report of the Department of Education.

2. Circulars of the Department of Education for 1873, 1874, and 1875.

3. Bulletins of the Department of Education for 1874 and 1875.

4. Tables of Educational Statistics for 1873 and 1874. English translation.

5. Report of Tanaka Fujimaro upon Education in Foreign Countries.

4. REGULATIONS OF GOVERNMENT SCHOOLS.

1. Calendar, etc., of the University of Tokio.

2. Regulations of the Tokio Medical College.

3. Regulations of the English-Language Schools at Tokio, Aichi, Osaka, Hiroshima, Nagasaki, Niigata, and Miyagi.

4. Regulations of the Normal Schools at Tokio, Aichi, Osaka, Hiroshima, Nagasaki, Niigata, and Miyagi.

5. Regulations of the Tokio Female School.

6. Regulations of the Tokio Female Normal School.

5. Charts, Maps, Books, and Apparatus for Schools.

1. Five Charts for teaching Language.
2. Six Charts for teaching Arithmetic.
3. Four Charts of Object-Lessons and Gymnastics
4. Five Species of Writing-Books.
5. Elementary Reading and Spelling Books.
6. Text-books on Elementary and General Geography.
7. Text-books on Elementary Arithmetic.
8. Outline of the History of Japan.
9. Outline of General History.
10. Drawing-Books.
11. Outline Map and Map of the World.
12. Five Charts on Natural History.
13. Balloon Globe.
14. Drawing-Slates.
15. Varieties of the Japanese Counting-Frame.
16. Varieties of School Slates.
17. Lacquered Slates.
18. School Desks and Chairs.
19. School apparatus manufactured at the Department of Arts and Manufactures of the University of Tokio, viz.: Polariscope, hydraulic ram, elliptical compass, glass-cutting machine, Newton's plates, plane mirrors, model of steam-engine, pyrometer, conjugate mirrors, sonometer, tuning-fork, force-pump, suction-pump, Magdeburg hemispheres, air-pump, Archimedes's screw, reaction wheel, hydraulic press, Cartesian diver, inclined plane, pulleys, wheel and axle, lever, concave mirror and convex mirror, double cone and inclined plane, rocking-toy, collision-balls, camera-obscura, centrifugal machine, adhesion plates, parallelogram of forces, gyroscope, orrery, wedge—accompanied by a list with prices.

6. Examination-Papers of Government Schools.

1. Examination-Papers of the University of Tokio.
2. Examination-Papers of the Tokio Foreign-Language School.
3. Examination-Paper of the English-Language Schools at Tokio, Aichi, Hiroshima, Nagasaki, Osaka, Niigata, and Miyagi.

APPENDIX.

4. Examination-Papers of the Normal Schools at Aichi, Osaka, Hiroshima, Nagasaki, Niigata, and Miyagi.
5. Examination-Papers of the Tokio Female School.
6. Examination-Papers of the school in Kumagai Ken.

7. KINDERGARTEN MATERIAL.

The collection under this head embraces forty-one different articles. They consist of boxes of letters, cards, puzzle-frames, etc.; of pictures, play-cards, easy-readers, simple games, shadow-pictures, hand-balls, and children's toys, together with four boxes of Kindergarten gifts.

8. LIBRARY, MUSEUM, AND BOTANICAL GARDEN.

1. Photographs of the Tokio Public Library.
2. Historical Account of the Tokio Public Library.
3. Regulations and Catalogue of the Tokio Public Library.
4. Historical Account of the Tokio Museum.
5. Map of the Botanical Garden.
6. Historical Account and Catalogue of the Botanical Garden.

9. DESIGNS AND PHOTOGRAPHS OF SCHOOLS.

1. Photographs and Plans of the University of Tokio.
2. Plans of the Tokio Medical College.
3. Plan of the Tokio Foreign-Language School.
4. Photographs and Plans of the English-Language Schools at Tokio, Aichi, Osaka, Hiroshima, Nagasaki, and Niigata.
5. Photographs and Plans of the Normal Schools at Tokio, Aichi, Osaka, Hiroshima, Nagasaki, Niigata, and Miyagi.
6. Plans of the Tokio Female Normal School.
7. Photographs of the Tokio Female Normal School.
8. Photographs and Plans of Schools in Kioto, Tokio, Tsuruga, Gifu, Osaka, and Hamamatsu.
9. Model of the Lecture-room of the old College of Confucius, at Tokio.
10. Plan of the old College-grounds.
11. Photographs of the Lecture-room.
12. Photographs of the Memorial Temple of Confucius, belonging to the College.

13. Photographs of the Statues of Confucius and Four of his Disciples, in the Memorial Temple.

14. Plan of the Ashikaga College at Kanazawa.

15. Plans of the Buildings and Grounds of the old Colleges at Okiyama, together with an Historical Account.

16. Plans of the Buildings and Grounds established by the Daimio of Mito.

10. BOOKS, MAPS, ETC.

Dictionaries.

1. Koyekikuai Giokuhen, a dictionary of arts.
2. Gorui Setzuyo-Shin, a dictionary.
3. Goi, a dictionary.
4. English-and-Japanese dictionary.

Histories.

5. Dai-Nipponshi: History of Great Japan, in one hundred volumes.
6. Ruijukokushi.
7. Nippongaishi: History of Japan, in twelve volumes.
8. Kinseijijou: Historical Narrative of Modern Japan, in seven volumes.
9. Jingu Seitoki: History of the Lineal Descendants of the Empress of Japan from the Empress Jingu, six volumes.
10. Bukonempio: Chronicle of the Tokugawa Government, eight volumes.
11. Shogun Kafu: Historical Account of the Several Dynasties of Shoguns, seven volumes.
12. Hankuanpu: History of the Japanese Daimios, twenty volumes.
13. Naigai-ichiran: Facts in Japanese History, Domestic and Foreign.

Maps.

14. Map of Japan from practical surveys, published by the Department of Education.
15. Records of the practical survey of Japan.
16. New Map of the World, with accompanying explanations.
17. Map of the Provinces and Districts of Japan.
18. Map of Japan, showing the different roads.
19. Large Map of Japan, by Nakafuru Teikio.
20. Map of the Grand-School Districts of Japan.

APPENDIX.

21. Map of the Grand-School Districts of Japan, with the names in English.

22. Pictures of Celebrated Mountains.

23. Maps of the Cities of Tokio, Kioto, and Osaka.

24. Maps of the Harbors of the Open Ports, Yokohama, Kobe, Nagasaki, Niigata, and Hakodate.

25. Maps published by the Hydrographic Bureau of the Navy Department, to wit, Kamaisi harbor, Bay of Notsuke, Miyaka harbor, Sutsu harbor, Otaru harbor, Hakodate harbor, Simoda harbor, Bay of Tokio, Bay of Goyoi, Straits Tsugaru, Sazara harbor, Yamagawa harbor, and chart of the inland sea of Satsuma and Osumi.

26. Maps of Yayeyama Island, Nemuro harbor, Sappo harbor, Unten harbor, Island of Amami.

27. Map of the School-Districts of the Cities and Provinces.

Laws, Ceremonies, etc.

28. Sinritsukorei and Kaiteiritsurei : new and improved criminal code.

29. Kenporuihen : collection of constitutional laws published by the Department of Justice, forty-eight volumes.

30. Yengisiki : book of ceremonies, sixty-one volumes.

Old Medical Books.

31. Isinho, thirty volumes.
32. Didoruijuho, ten volumes.
33. Giniho, three volumes.
34. Kenshuroku.
35. Yokuahitsuroku, ten volumes.
36. Riodigawa, two volumes.
37. Kuishi, three volumes.
38. Seikushoku.
39. Manyu-Zasshi, two volumes.

Botanical Books.

40. Yamato-honzo, twenty-five volumes.
41. Ko-yamato-honzo, twelve volumes.
42. Honzo Yaku Meibiko.
43. Honzo Tsukuan, fifty-five volumes.

44. Somoku Bengi, four volumes.
45. Honzo Wamei, two volumes.

Books of Verses, Ancient and Modern.

46. Dakuan Roeishin, four volumes.
47. Manyo Wakashin, twenty volumes.
48. Rikikashin, two volumes.
49. Ruidai Soyashin, twelve volumes.
50. Kochobun Ruimeikazekku, three volumes.
51. Kocho Meikashisho, nine volumes.
52. Kokinshin Tokagami, six volumes.
53. Meirinkashin, five volumes.

Books of Prose, Ancient and Modern.

54. Honcho Bunsai, fifteen volumes.
55. Fuso Shomeishin, three volumes.
56. Kinsei meika bunsho, eight volumes.

Japanese and Chinese Styles of Writing.

57. Eight books, showing different kinds of writing, consisting in all of forty volumes.

Books of Music.

58. Twenty-one volumes on music, ancient and modern.

Biographies of Celebrated Persons.

59. Fifty-four volumes, consisting of biographies of Chinese and Japanese heroes and sages.

Books concerning Natural History and Agriculture.

60. One hundred and fourteen volumes, descriptive of the agriculture and the natural history of Japan.
61. Tables of botanical classification, published by the Department of Education.
62. Tables showing the strength of Japanese timber, published by the University of Tokio, from practical experiments.

Almanacs.

63. Almanac for the fifth year of Ansei.
64. Almanacs for the fourth and sixth years of Meiji.

APPENDIX. 197

65. Solar Almanac for the eighth year of Meiji.
66. Solar and Lunar Almanac.

Old Model Books of Writing for Children.

67. I-ro-ha, numerals and sentences.
68. Writing-books, showing the modes of writing family names, first letters of names, different names of provinces, the different directions in Yedo, and various commercial expressions.
69. Books showing the styles of writing letters, letter-writing for girls, etc.

Lectures and Treatises.

70. Rika Nikka, Journal of Physics, published by the Department of Education, twenty-four volumes.
71. Nikko Kibun, daily lectures published by the Department of Education, eleven volumes.
72. Lectures of Nishimura Shigeki before a Private School, nine volumes.
73. Journal of the Meirokusha, a society of scholars, forty-one numbers.
74. Journal of the Tokio Medical College.
75. Records of Medical Operations by the Tokio Medical College, eleven volumes.
76. A Complete Medical Treatise by the Tokio Medical College, four volumes.

Old Arithmetical Books.

77. Seiho Jinkoki, by Bunkaido.
78. Daizen Ginkoki, by Hasegawa Zenyemon and Yamamoto Yasunosin.
79. Sanpo Sinsho, by Hasegawa Zenyemon and Chiba Yuhichi.
80. Sampo Kiuseki Tsuko, by Hasegawa Zenyemon and Uchida Hango, five volumes.

Catalogues of New Books.

81. List of Publications for the Fourth Year of Meiji (1871).
82. Lists of Publications for the Sixth and Seventh Years of Meiji (1873-1874).
83. List of New Publications.

II. NEWSPAPERS.

1. Historical account of newspapers.
2. Mosiogusa, part thirty-two.

3. Yenkin Shimbun, twenty-one copies.
4. Chiugai Shimbun, four copies.
5. Kosi Zappo, ten copies.
6. Naigai Sinpozenki, seven copies.
7. Naigai Sinpo, forty-four copies.
8. Nichiyo Shimbun, seven copies.
9. Tokio Nichi Nichi Shimbun for March, 1875.
10. Yokohama Mainichi Shimbun for June, 1875.
11. Akebono Shimbun for June, 1875.
12. Hachi Shimbun for May, 1875.
13. Yomi-uri Shimbun for May, 1875.
14. Nisshin Shinjishi for June, 1875.
15. Hirakana Yeiri Shimbun, illustrated, for September, 1875.
16. Saifu Shimbun for January, 1876.
17. Makoto Shimbun, six copies.
18. Kanoyomi Shimbun, fourteen copies.
19. Hananomi Yako-onna Shimbun, sixteen copies.

12. INSTRUMENTS, APPARATUS, AND LITERARY MATERIAL.

Medical Instruments, Modern.

1. A collection of instruments used for modern surgery, made in Japan, consisting of microscopes, eye-instruments, ear-instruments, specula, galvano-caustic apparatus, curved dressing-tins, etc., etc., in all consisting of twenty-seven varieties.
2. One box amputating-instruments, seventy kinds.
3. One box surgical instruments, twenty-one kinds.
4. One set of dental instruments, three kinds.
5. Electric explorer for gunshot-wounds.
6. Splints, three varieties.

Medicines and Medical Instruments, Ancient.

7. Medical chest with medicines and instruments, with directions for use.
8. One hundred and eighty-four varieties of old Japanese and Chinese medicines, collected by the Tokio Medical College.

APPENDIX. 199

Measuring-Instruments.

9. Five varieties of protractor.
10. Three varieties of quadrant.
11. Sun-dial furnished with compass, and other sun-dials.
12. Mariner's compass, circumferenters' compasses.
13. Scales of wood and brass, calipers, measuring-chains, bamboo scales, metre-scales, surveyors' scales, etc.
14. Instruments for measuring dry and liquid substances.
15. Clock, pendulum, barometer, etc.
16. Balances.

Globes.

17. Large globe, by Hashitsume Kuanichi, Tokio.
18. Medium-sized globe, by the same.
19. Small globe, by Matsui Tadatosi.

Ancient Writing-Instruments.

20. Writing-table.
21. Inkstone-box, accompanied with ink, pens, water-pot, pen-holder, etc.
22. Table, gold-lacquered with cherry-tree on a pear-colored ground.
23. Inkstone-box, gold-lacquered with cherry-blossoms, accompanied with a silver water-pot.
24. Pen-box, gold-lacquered with pine-tree and monkeys on a black ground.
25. Literary box, gold-lacquered with pine-tree and long-tailed birds.
26. Paper box, gold-lacquered with pine-tree and the plant tachibana.
27. Inkstone-box, lacquered with pine-tree and tachibana, with pen-holder, knife, ink-holder, awl, and water-pot.
28. Book-shelf, gold-lacquered with snow-figures and ivies.
29. Writing-table, with two drawers.
30. Large inkstone, with wooden stand.
31. Inkstone, with cover and stand.
32. Ivory pen-box, crystal pen-box, crystal ink-rest, crystal washing-pot, crystal pen-rest.
33. Pocket inkstone, box, knife, awl, etc.
34. Pocket red inkstone-box.

35. Portable ink-cases.
36. Newspaper-holders.

Arithmetical Counting-Frames.

37. Abacus, with twenty-five sliding wires.
38. Abacus, made of oak, with twenty-one wires.
39. Abacus, of black persimmon, with fifteen wires.
40. Abacus, after the European style.
41. Pocket paper abacus.

Pencils or Brushes.

42. Six varieties of pencils manufactured in Bizen.
43. Ten varieties of pencils manufactured in Shinano.
44. Six varieties of pencils manufactured in Tokio.

Paper.

45. Eighty-one varieties of paper manufactured in Japan, including plain writing-paper, heavy paper, gold and silver paper, fancy paper for poetry, etc.

Pen-holders.

46. Twenty-four styles of pen-holders, including plain bamboo, tortoise-shell, gilt and lacquered, etc.

Inks.

47. Nineteen varieties of ink in hard cakes, like India-ink.

Books for Memoranda and Accounts.

48. Twenty-one varieties of books, partly in the ancient style, and partly bound and ruled in the modern style.

13. PAINTING AND PAINTING-INSTRUMENTS.

1. Pictures illustrative of medical science, by Kondo Shobi, Tokio Medical College, twenty sheets.
2. Picture showing the mode of refining gold and silver in the Sado Mines, by Kitatsume Yukei.
3. Picture of football, three sheets.
4. Picture of Bingono Samuro, by Kikuchi Yosai (modern).
5. Picture of a farm-house, by Takahisa Aigan (modern).
6. Picture of a pine-tree, by Chinzan (modern).

7. Picture of Gengi, by Kano Shosenin (modern).
8. Picture of musical dance, by Sumiyoshi Naiki (modern).
9. Picture of first attacking warriors on the river Uji, by Kano Isenin (modern).
10. Picture of flowers, birds, and man (modern).
11. Picture of woman (modern).
12. Picture of flowers, birds, grasses, and trees (modern).

Raised Pictures.

13. Tablet representing the plucking of tea-leaves.
14. Tablet of a plum-tree with orioles.
15. Tablet of an elephant.
16. Tablet of the battle of Okeha Sama.
17. Tablet of Kusunoki (an ancient general) parting with his son.
18. Tablet of a farm-house.
19. Tablet of the poetess Komachi washing a leaf of a book of poems.
20. A fan representing the poet Yukihira.
21. A fan representing the poetess Chiyo.
22. A fan representing the dance of Chiyo.
23. A fan representing the poet Tosihira.
24. A fan representing the Bonaderi, a kind of dance.
25. A fan representing a trades-woman.

Lacquered Pictures.

26. Tablet of Jingukuogu.
27. Tablet of Kato Kiyomasa, an ancient hero.
28. Tablet of Kuanou, a Chinese general.
29. Tablet of the sago-palm, with frogs.
30. Tablet of a falcon.
31. Tablet of Fugiyama.
32. Treatise on lacquer-painting, by Sakakibara Yosino, Tokio.
33. Translation of the above, by Takahashi Korekiyo, Tokio.

Instruments for Drawing and Painting.

34. Twelve varieties of drawing-instruments for geometrical drawing.
35. One box containing painting-instruments and paints, in all seventy-eight articles.

36. Instruments for lacquer-pictures, consisting of pencils, whetstones, charcoal, lacquer, etc., in all twenty-three different articles.

Engraving and Engraving-Instruments.

37. Specimens of wood-engraving, plain and colored.
38. Lithographic pictures.
39. Engraving upon copper.
40. Table for wood-engraving.
41. Box of instruments for wood-engraving, brushes, mallets, etc.
42. Wooden blocks for engraving Chinese or Japanese books, blocks on which are engraved the Japanese syllabary, flowers, and birds.
43. Instruments for printing, consisting of brushes for colored inks, stand for moistening paper, inks of different varieties, etc.

14. PHOTOGRAPHS.

1. Photographs taken by Uchida Kuichi, Tokio, viz.: Yenriokuwan, Imperial Seaside Resort; Imperial Garden in Kioto; Tombs of the Tokugawa Family, Tokio; Views of the Gates of the Imperial Palace, Tokio; Views of Temples, Bridges, etc., in Tokio; Views in Nagasaki, Yokohama, Kobe, and Osaka.

2. Photographs taken by Shimidzu Tokoku, viz.: Views of the Imperial Palace; Views of Temples, Gates, Buildings, Bridges, etc., in Tokio.

www.ingramcontent.com/pod-product-compliance
Lightning Source LLC
Chambersburg PA
CBHW020918230426
43666CB00008B/1486